RECONSTRUCTING ECCLESIA

Is there a future for the church?

David W. Hewitt

Foreword by John Crowder

Wellsprings Community

FIRST PUBLISHED 2022 | THIRD EDITION 2024
Wellsprings Community
ISBN 978-1-7392680-0-8
Wellsprings Community, 71 Whitehill Street, Newcraighall, Edinburgh EH21 8QZ

Permissions

Wellsprings Community is a registered Scottish charity SC040639

ACKNOWLEDGEMENTS

The front cover design was produced by the author, inspired by Rublev's 1425 ikon of the Trinity.

Thone Hupa and Christopher Hewitt finalised the cover layout.

The rear cover includes an extract from Fra Angelico 'The Forerunners of Christ with Saints and Martyrs' 1423-4.

Grateful thanks are given to Matt Spinks and Ivan Schmid for contributing examples of church communities, and to the Northumbria Community for initially inspiring the Celtic liturgies and offices (see Appendix)

Dedicated to my wife Maggie,
my precious partner in the Great Adventure

Contents

1

FOREWORD

by John Crowder

The great exodus we now witness from the church's pews is indeed a largely noble iconoclasm. Infrequently railing against the ancient faith itself (which is rarely articulated or embodied well enough to be sufficiently rejected), but against lifeless wineskins of Western modernity, religious transactionalism and encrusted hierarchies of fear and control which promulgate an anaemic version of 'god' who little resembles Jesus Christ.

Deconstruction has its place as a necessary birth pang, but it is likewise *ignoble* to the degree its disillusionments are informed by stereotypes and endemic bitterness that polarize and further divide rather than grasp for a higher unity beyond differences. A unity found in Christ alone. We are all victims. We have all victimized ... the church is comprised of *humans*. Nevertheless, our healing also comes through openness and vulnerability with others in relation.

Though our rugged individualism tempts us to retreat in isolation, community must not be abandoned but reimagined. In this paper, David Hewitt – who we've nicknamed the 'Archbishop of Edinburgh' – aims to recover a vision for the beautiful, messy, bread-breaking struggle and vibrancy of doing life together in communion. A church not idealized, but as she is ... for as long as we idolize some pristine notion of flawless community, we end up missing the real humans in front of us, with all their myriad of faults, quirks and eccentricities.

'To love at all is to be vulnerable. Love anything and your heart will be wrung and possibly broken,' writes C.S. Lewis. 'If you want to make sure of keeping it intact you must give it to no one, not even an animal. Wrap it carefully round with hobbies and little luxuries; avoid all entanglements. Lock it up safe in the casket or coffin of your selfishness. But in that casket, safe, dark, motionless, airless, it will change. It will not be broken; it will become unbreakable, impenetrable, irredeemable. To love is to be vulnerable.'

The call to community is a call to love. If we are to speak of the church's reconstruction to come ... let us tremble lest we aim at cobbling together yet another idol that will again require toppling. The church needs *resurrection*. If she is to be built, it is by the hands and word of Christ. If she is to spread, it will be not by growth models but by contagious hearts once again on fire with Triune love. We do not need more tools, gifts or charisma ... we need *wonder.*

Jaroslov Pelikan often said, 'Tradition is the living faith of the dead; traditionalism is the dead faith of the living.'

The church is exhausted with innovating new packages. There is rest in returning to a pure, ageless Gospel of grace. We must become obsessed not with *form*, whether ancient or contemporary, but with our Former. In an age of consumerism, our slick new means of marketing and polishing dysfunction only weary those window shopping for the perfect church (rest assured you would ruin that perfect church if you ever found it!).

We are the church. In all our sublime brokenness, we were never called to build anything but to *be something* ... but to be something *together*. An incarnate community in witness, embodying the kenotic, other-giving love of Christ. The paradox and wonder is His apocalyptic in-breaking and redemption in the very midst all our chaotic blundering.

In fact, St. Gregory of Nyssa writes, 'Now the body of Christ, as I have often said, is the whole of humanity.' The church is not a separated microcosm of humanity, but she is a distinct *sacrament* of Christ within this hurting world, awakening all people to the unconditional acceptance and loving inclusion of our Father.

To articulate this clearly, assuredly we need fewer teachers and more fathers. 'Archbishop' David is just such a father - a dear friend of many years, a man of passion and wisdom who embodies deep humility and joy ... his work here is a valuable contribution to the dire need for a living ecclesiology.

John Crowder, Portland USA 2022

INTRODUCTION

Having been born into a traditional, British middle-class Anglican church-going family in the mid 1950s, my outlook could have remained fairly narrow and unconventional. However, my life journey, taking me to Scotland, to Africa, and through several different versions of Christian faith, has led me to a very different place in my understanding. In some things I have come full circle. In others, my twenty-something self would not recognise me now.

I have always loved a sense of community and of common purpose. I was impacted early on by Lesslie Newbigin's work on cultural relevance in church and mission[1]; I have always felt that the ecclesia should display an exciting, vibrant expression in each generation. Creativity has been an abiding dynamic in my family: art, dance, music and percussion. Many have influenced me along the way – including Andy Au, Martin Neil, Colin Symes and Rupert Ward – and to all I'm profoundly grateful; the Mirror Word paraphrase by Francois du Toit and the songs of Godfrey Birtill have also been particularly significant in this. An interest in the Celtic church has always been there, but in more recent years a greater clarity about an indispensable Trinitarian faith and the message of grace has awakened my excitement about the gospel. For this I'm indebted to John Crowder and Dr Baxter Kruger.

---

[1] I heard Lesslie Newbigin speak in the 1970s in Birmingham. 'The Gospel is the truth, and therefore it is true for all men. It is the unveiling of the face of Him who makes all things, from whom every man comes, and to whom every man goes. It is the revealing of the meaning of human history, of the origin and destiny of mankind. Jesus is not only my Saviour, He is the Lord of all things, the cause and cornerstone of the universe.'

During the Covid pandemic I was aware of some close friends becoming disillusioned with church. Some of them have even walked away from the faith as we know it. While understanding some of the reasons people have been led to 'deconstruction', and fully appreciating their need for detox, when I have heard people say they reject *any* need for church, I've also felt a resounding 'No!' within.

To use a common saying, let's not throw the baby out with the bathwater. Yes, there's much of grime and soap suds to drain away ... but there is also a living body in there, born from above. It may at times be noisy, smelly and immature, but it is full of potential, carrying the parental DNA. Apparently, this baby-bathwater idiom derives from a German proverb, *das Kind mit dem Bade ausschütten* (recorded as early as 1512 and even used by Luther). Thomas Carlyle adapted the concept in an 1849 essay, 'Fling-out your dirty water with all zeal and set it careening down the kennels; but try, if you can, keep the little child!'

So, during those months of lockdown a paper was born: **Towards a new ecclesiology**, which forms Section One of this small book. After some additional reflection, Section Two develops those themes further. Section Three adds some contemporary examples (as it's always good to hear how things work out in practice). Finally, there are some contemplative offices in the appendices that people may find useful. Of course, this is not meant to be a final word on the subject. Much is a collation of ideas from others combined with my own processing. I'm aiming this at precious people who have given up on church or may feel it is just not important anymore, now that they are into 'grace'. Let us continue the conversation.

David Hewitt, Edinburgh 2022

ONE | TOWARDS A NEW ECCLESIOLOGY

In response to a question that I raised at a theological 'Whisky Retreat' on Islay in 2018, Dr Baxter Kruger observed that while the church is still important, we 'need a new ecclesiology.' This essay will consider this; the relevance or otherwise of church in the light of a renewed Trinitarian perspective, which affirms that all things are – and have always been – held together in Christ. That through the incarnation and the work of the Cross, the Son of God entered our darkness and our twisted, fallen state. Through his redeeming genius, the last Adam took the whole of mankind into death with him, in order that we might be made new in his resurrected life: a relationship restored with the Father who loves us! As Baxter states, 'The essential nature of the church is the fellowship of the astonished heart' – overwhelmed by the wonder of a God that is humble, patient and kind and crosses any obstacle to come to us, in unrelenting love.

In his dissertation for Aberdeen University, Baxter had written:

> To speak the name of Jesus Christ with the apostles, and with the early Church leaders is to say, 'Father's eternal and beloved Son,' and it is to say, 'Holy Spirit anointed One,' and it is to say, 'the Creator and Sustainer of all things – incarnate, crucified, resurrected, and ascended to the Father.'
>
> Therefore, to speak the name of Jesus is to say that the Father, the Holy Spirit, the human race, and all creation are not

separated, but together in relationship. Jesus is himself the relationship; he is the union between the Triune God and the human race. In him, heaven and earth, the life of the blessed Trinity and broken human life are united. Jesus is our new creation, our adoption, our inclusion in the divine life, the renewed covenant relationship between God and humanity, the kingdom of the Triune God on earth.[2]

Through this lens we must now see everything! In John 14:20 Jesus tells the disciples 'In that day you will know that I am in my Father, and you are in me, and I am in you.' In the light of his saving work, we are born from above into our eternal family. Even if people do not realise it – and most do not – Christ is dwelling in them, and they need to awaken to the reality of what he has done. He invites all to participate in this *perichoresis* 'circle dance' with the Godhead, to enjoy the benefits that, through grace, have been poured out freely upon us.

However, there are few things that stir up such a strong response these days as the term **'church'**! Caricatured in the media as bigoted, reactionary or 'just plain mean', it must be sadly admitted that our Christian culture has *sometimes* given blatant evidence for this poor image. The church today has been evacuated in droves by those that claim to have been hurt or misunderstood and disdained by those intent on 'deconstruction'. It is clear from falling church statistics that the notion of church as an institution is undergoing a seismic transformation. The COVID-19 pandemic – like previous plagues,

---

[2] Dr Baxter Kruger had the privilege of doing his doctoral dissertation on the theology of Professor T.F.Torrance, under the tutelage of his brother J.B.Torrance at King's College, Aberdeen.' T.F.Torrance was, in his opinion, 'the Athanasius of the modern West.'

persecutions and wars in history – accelerated the rate of change, with many people asking basic questions, re-evaluating the way they spend their time and reviewing the things that take up their focus. Young people – and not so young – are asking Why? How? When? and questioning the very basis of 'church'.

Why do we need churches anymore?

If then because of Christ we all have free access through the indwelling Spirit to an intimate, loving and enabling relationship, forgiven and set free from our bondage to our former harmful ways, what is the point of any formalised group or organisation termed church?

We do not need a priest or other cleric to intercede on our behalf, or any other intermediary: our great High Priest has fulfilled all that is necessary. Even though sacred spaces or traditional church settings may engender contemplation or offer welcome escape from the whirl of contemporary life – and are still valued by many as such – we know that they are not ultimately essential. Our faith is the faith of Christ: we do not need to depend on external forms to achieve any benefit. Liturgy, icons, candles and incense may be useful, but none are prescribed. Jesus makes it clear in John 4 that worship is not a matter of location, but of heart. Buildings should never be the issue!

In the world of evangelical or charismatic communities, other aspects come under scrutiny though. Usually built upon more conservative teaching, they may demand adherence to codes of behaviour, tithing, endless programmes and conferences, sometimes appearing as commercial and hierarchical as business corporations! Sadly, these very institutions can often become self-serving, requiring a regular inflow of finance just to keep afloat (particularly at the mega scale when large staff or TV ministry are involved). Some speak of the 'idolatrous distraction factor' of this type of church, with its concentric, empire ideologies, its sacred/secular divides, its retreat from involvement in ordinary everyday life.[3]

Sometimes it is easier to say what something is *not*, than what it *is*. Church should clearly not be about maintaining a Sunday facade, maintaining an outdated structure, preserving religious systems of control or brainwashing! Certainly not about architecture. It is also not meant to be a rigid, inward-looking institution or reactionary club. But Jesus and the apostles actually spoke of the church in positive ways, so what was Holy Spirit wanting to grow?

We must be aware of the presuppositions or biases we may bring to the discussion. If we are trying to protect something we are familiar with, we may be unduly cautious about a re-evaluation of church. If it is our livelihood, we may be overly defensive! Yet, at the other end of the scale, if we have been in the mode of 'deconstruction' we may resist any attempt to define it. Brad Jersak makes a valuable point when he comments that 'deconstruction' is a rather violent or clumsy term to use; after all, we are talking of the precious Body of Christ here. Maybe reformation or 'healing' would be a better way of approaching the subject? It should be noted also that this discussion relates to a Western context; there may be other factors that are specific to different cultures.

---

[3] Michael Lafleur in Toronto has vocalised these shortcomings and stressed the need to deconstruct and reimagine church.

What does 'church' really mean?

The Greek word *ekklesia* was in common usage at the time the New Testament was being written down as an 'assembly' or gathering of citizens in society. The Greek city-state involved bringing people together to discuss and govern, and many immediately point to this. Yet, it had its limitations – even at the height of Greek democracy, only full citizens had the right to say anything in the *ekklesia*; aliens or slaves had no right. Some scholars note that this is not the only way this word is used: in the Septuagint – the second century BC Greek translation of the Old Testament scriptures made by rabbis fully conversant in Hebrew and Greek, and the version Jesus and the apostles most regularly quote from – the term *'assembly* of Israel' (Hebrew *qahal*) is mostly also translated *ekklesia*, particularly in connection to them gathering around the covenant. This is more likely what was in their minds than a Greek societal structure![4] See also Acts 7:23-39 where Stephen equates church with being Israel, the 'congregation in the desert'.

If Israel was the 'womb of the incarnation'[5] then they did not see the church as a 'new institution' but rather a continuation and fulfilment of all God intended to reveal through his Son, the manifest body of Christ on earth.

The nature of the *ekklesia* that Jesus was bringing about was to have many differences from a political one; it would be set apart (only by grace) in his holiness but inclusive and open for all. It would be built

---

[4] Where the Masoretic Text uses the term *qahal*, the Septuagint (LXX) usually uses the Koine Greek term *ekklesia*, ἐκκλησία, which means "summoned group" (literally, "they who are called out").
[5] T.F Torrance, drawing on Karl Barth

on the revelation of who he is. Remember Simon Peter's declaration at Caesarea Philippi:

> Now when Jesus came into the region of Caesarea Philippi, He was asking His disciples, "Who do people say that the Son of Man is?" ..... Simon Peter answered, "You are the Christ, the Son of the living God." And Jesus said to him, "Blessed are you, Simon Barjona, because flesh and blood did not reveal this to you, but My Father who is in heaven. And I also say to you that you are Peter [*stone*], and upon this rock [*bedrock*] I will build My church; and the gates of Hades [*the realm of the dead*] will not overpower it.[6]

Caesarea Philippi was known for Banias, a collection of springs and pagan worship sites linked to the cult of Pan. He was the Greco-Roman god of nature, livestock, hunting, etc. — all things related to wild times, party music, and, of course, fertility. You can still see the remains of it today — I have stood there — and the centrepiece of this ancient worship site is a huge cliff and grotto, which contain the remains of numerous altars, caves, temples, and courtyards. The entire area teemed with Roman mythology and idolatry. What Jesus was building was going to be in stark contrast to this darkness of human superstition and the pernicious world systems that locked people in death — rather, it would be the Life that the Godhead had intended from the start, a shared cruciform life that would be characterised by resurrection. 'The church was not founded as a theological institution—it was founded as a community that had an encounter with Jesus.'[7]

---

[6] Matthew 16:13, 16-18 New American Standard Bible®, Copyright © 1960, 1971, 1977, 1995, 2020 by The Lockman Foundation. All rights reserved. Notes added.
[7] Dr Baxter Kruger, Introducing the Trinitarian Faith 2020

Francois du Toit comments that *ekklesia* derives from **ek**, a preposition denoting origin, and **kelsia** from **kaleo**, to surname, thus speaking of our original identity.[8] Thus he says the church is Christ's redeemed image and likeness in human form. It would be a loving community, as alluded to in his Upper Room discourses (John 13:35), and one in which matters would be conducted with fairness and transparency, in a mode of grace (Matt 18:15-17). But it would ultimately be as new wine requiring new wine skins, incarnating the Risen Lord on the earth:

> And the church is his body; it is made full and complete by Christ, who fills all things everywhere with himself.[9]

> The Ekklesia is his body. The completeness of his being that fills all in all resides in us! God cannot make himself more visible or exhibit himself more accurately.[10]

It would not be the narrow, insular faith of one nation, but the fulfilment of God's promise to Abraham that through him 'all families of the earth will be blessed' (Gen 12:1-3).

Though we find the term *ekklesia* only recorded twice on Jesus lips, it could be argued he alluded to it many times, and when it comes to the rest of the New Testament it appears 112 more times in singular or plural form.

---

[8] Notes on Ekklesia in the Mirror Study Bible, p.503-504 referring to Matthew 16:13-19 in commentary on Revelation.

[9] Ephesians 1:23 New Living Translation, copyright © 1996, 2004, 2015 by Tyndale House Foundation.

[10] Ephesians 1:23 Mirror Bible (paraphrase by Francois du Toit)

In particular, the Apostle Paul teaches much in connection to *ekklesia,* seeing the church ultimately as a prophetic vessel through which 'the manifold wisdom of God should be made known to the rulers and authorities in the heavenly realms ...' (Eph 3:10 NIV). 'The church acts like a prism that disperses the varied magnitude of God in human form.'[11]

Paul and the other apostle apparently travelled around the ancient world recognising gatherings of believers as examples of *ekklesia,* establishing a simple format for functioning with *presbuteros* (elders) and diaconate (servers). While we cannot point to any exact blueprint for church, it's clear that these were relational gatherings of believers led by trusted individuals, who were able to teach and encourage these nascent communal expressions amid a pagan and often hostile world.

Some people today are teaching that as all are made perfect in Christ (Heb 10.14), then all humanity should be considered 'church'. Certainly, all are included in Christ's finished work – the Saviour of the World (Gk. *cosmos*) – and there are now no more 'hoops to jump through' to enter in, but does that view really stack up with the witness of the New Testament writers? It seems to me that they had in mind something wonderful, something loving and lifegiving, a community that is joined to the Head and delights to *demonstrate* this awareness of redeemed life with a world still asleep. Nevertheless, the message proclaimed is indeed a 'Global Gospel'.[12]

---

[11] Ephesians 3:10b Mirror Bible (paraphrase by Francois du Toit)

[12] Francois du Toit favours this term, rather than suggestions of 'universalism' that is so often misunderstood. An authentic Christology holds fast to the uniqueness of Jesus Christ but acknowledges that he is the 'lamb that takes away the sins of the world.'

A brief historical overview

We have to acknowledge, however, that the track record of the *ekklesia* is a mixed bag. After a vibrant period of meeting in homes and gathering together in the Temple courts, the early church became scattered with the waves of persecution that followed. Yet during the first 300 years the Good News was received gladly by gentile converts throughout the Roman Empire, and the fulfilment of Genesis 12 that 'all nations would be blessed' was beginning to be seen. New expressions of *ekklesia* began to emerge throughout Asia Minor and the ancient world.

However, the early centuries were marked by competing influences, whether from those that would try to turn the clock back to legalism – such as the Judaizers – or those that would seek to shroud it in secrecy – such as the Gnostics – or those like the Arians who would seek to diminish Jesus' status to less than God. There was also a significant split between Jewish and gentile believers …. something that seems in conflict with New Testament teaching (e.g. Ephesians Chapter 2).

It took the Council of Nicaea in 325AD – with insights from such as the young Athanasius – to thrash out the Creed, clarifying the Trinitarian relationship of Father, Son and Spirit. Interestingly the Nicene Creed also began to acknowledge the importance of 'the holy catholic and apostolic church' (more fully adopted in 381) as being the reliable, ongoing vehicle for sharing this, a faith held in common with the cloud of witnesses that had gone before.

Sadly, although the Emperor Constantine's conversion brought an end to the waves of persecution (and it was he who had called together the Council of Nicaea) many regard this as another fault line in the historical church, in which state involvement began to institutionalise what had begun as a relational network. In Rome, empire and religion were as one, and this approach was transferred to the *ekklesia*. In towns and cities across the empire, basilicas had been buildings where legal matters were resolved and business transactions carried out. Architecturally, they were imposing structures; rectangular buildings split into aisles by columns and covered by a roof, often with an apse at one end. These now became adopted as 'churches' for the new state religion – setting a style in ecclesiastical architecture that has continued, with some variations, down through the centuries. Powerful symbols of state religion.

Church government in the Roman Empire also espoused a hierarchical, centralised system. This had even been developing in the second century. Christ's very affirmation of Peter was taken to sanction a religious organisation concentrated on the Holy See in Rome. Undoubtedly there were many men and women of great integrity and faith, but sadly this now combined with the use of basilicas and other symbols of status to engender a more formal, legalistic shape to the emerging faith.

Not all branches of *ekklesia* were the same though. We can see how the Celtic church – influenced by the Desert Fathers – developed along more organic, monastic lines. Apparently, there are links from the church in Ephesus directly to the Celtic church in Wales (186 AD) – bypassing Rome altogether.

The Ephesian church was in fact shaped by the Apostles John, Paul and Timothy, and with later links to Polycarp (Jerome wrote that Polycarp was a "disciple of the apostle John and by him ordained

presbyter of Smyrna"). Along with other Celts like Hilary of Poitiers –
it was from these roots in the early centuries that grew the more
relational Celtic church movements led by Saints Patrick, Columba,
Aiden and the like in Ireland and across the British Isles. These strands
have continued up to the present day.

Sadly, at the Synod of Whitby 664 AD – due to political expediency –
the Celtic church was largely subsumed into the Roman tradition.[13]
The East-West split in the Middle Ages (from 1054 AD) saw the
Orthodox churches, centred on Constantinople, become distinct from
the Roman Catholic. We were in a period when 'Christendom' implied
that Christianity could be imposed through the state, leading to such
aberrations as the Crusades or the religious wars that would tear
Europe apart.

The Protestant Reformation then emerged from 1517 AD, when a
German monk called Martin Luther took issue with the beliefs and
practices of the Catholic Church. John Calvin gave us a reformed
theology based on personal faith, and the invention of the printing
press, alongside many translations of the Bible in people's mother
tongue, swung the balance away from the domination of the
historical churches.

Yet, in the 500 years since, Protestantism has splintered into many
denominations.[14] The Pentecostal and Charismatic movements of the

---

[13] Ray Simpson points out that 'Others argue that the influence of the Synod of
Whitby has been grossly inflated: it affected just one Anglo-Saxon kingdom, and
its central decision, to unify the date of Easter, was no more than common sense.'
Celtic Christianity and Climate Crisis, Sacristy Press 2020
[14] Though sometimes cited as 40-50,000 this figure is hardly credible and seems to
cite the same denomination as separate if in different countries, or, for example,
variations of Baptist as all separate. The authoritative Pew Research Center

20th Century, while demonstrating a dynamic enlarging and revitalising of the church, have in turn spawned many and varied expressions. These have added colour and life to the worldwide church, restoring the power and immediacy of the Spirit. Yet some have in turn developed new megachurch empires that have not always been healthy for their adherents, with quite large 'revolving doors' in which some gravitate back to more traditional churches, and others walk away altogether.

More recently, appalling revelations of misuse, control, historical sexual abuse etc have emerged in some quarters. Of course, this is not confined to the church, but when it occurs there it has added to a sense of hypocrisy and caused many to question the very basis of the faith. Yet as people have revised their understanding of history, perhaps much is also conflated in a stream of zealous 'woke' ideas and 'cancel culture'. Missionary movements, heroes of the faith and the spreading of Christianity have been lumped in with western imperialism, exploitation and insensitivity. Nevertheless, we should not underplay the damage that was done at times by the church:

> That sense of rightness can inoculate us against humility, infusing us in an excessive confidence or addiction to certainty that keeps us from seeing our mistakes until after the harm has been done – to others (including our children) and to ourselves. *Our religion is right*, we believe, *which makes us right*. As a result, the more devoted we are, the more

compiled a list of major Protestant denominations in 2015, which when whittled down to main groupings, seems to be around 200. Beyond that there are of course many non-denominational groups. Article by Stephen Beale, National Catholic Register 31 Oct 2017

stubborn and unteachable we become. And everyone can see it but us, because we're blinded by our sincerity and zeal.[15]

Indigenous people, from all the great continents of the world, were sometimes treated as 'less than' human image-bearers of the Lord. There were many notable exceptions though, with missionaries who were able to integrate with other races and separate cultural distinctives from the essential gospel message. While it is good that we review history in the light of new understanding, we need to be careful not to be too quick to judge former generations by the values of today.

The reality is that the *ekklesia* has always been made up of people who were broken and damaged (who has not been damaged to some extent?) who have lived in the dark, but now encountered the Light. It is only the Saviour of the World (lit. *cosmos*) who heals this. Jesus spent much time among the hurting in society, saying 'Who goes to the doctor for a cure? Those who are well or those who are sick? I have not come to call the 'righteous,' but those who are sinners and bring them to repentance.'[16] If history shows us anything, it is that church is messy because people are messy:

> Churches are living rooms, and if the persons living in them are sinners, there will be clothes scattered about, handprints on the woodwork, and mud on the carpet. For as long as Jesus insists on calling sinners and not the righteous to repentance, churches are going to be an embarrassment to the fastidious and an affront to the upright... They are simply lampstands

---

[15] Brian McLaren in his book Do I *stay* Christian? (p.16 Hodder & Stoughton 2022)
[16] Mark 2:17 The Passion Translation®. Copyright © 2017, 2018, 2020 by Passion & Fire Ministries, Inc.

where the light of Christ is shown. They are not themselves the light... there must be no idealisation of the church, and lament ought to be restrained. Eulogy and anguish are misplaced ...[the churches] were never much better or much worse than they are today. They just are.[17]

What then is the heart of *ekklesia*?

From its humble beginnings like a simple fishing boat carried by the wind, it seems sometimes that the church has morphed into a vast container ship, set on fixed courses, running on dirty fuel oil, very slow to turn around and encrusted with barnacles and weeds en route. Why not just abandon ship and simply relate to God ourselves, when and how we want to?

However, rather than dismiss the church as irrelevant today, maybe we should ask other questions. What were the essential characteristics of the vessels Jesus and the apostles intended us to sail in?

The problem with discussions such as these is that we tend to project back the present-day understanding we have of church 2,000 years. The basic reality then was very different. Jesus preached the Kingdom – he had very little to say about the church. The assembly (what *ekklesia* means) was simply the community involved in a movement – Kingdom meaning something like 'revolution'. Church was meant to be family – and what Christians were involved in was 'the Way'. Until the

---

[17] Eugene H. Peterson in Reversed Thunder: The Revelation of John and the Praying Imagination (1991)

latter part of the 1st Century this was the pattern. As the apostles died there was radical change. The gospel of grace was no longer understood, and 'church' became religion and organisation – and absorbed some very strange ideas. That was all before church buildings ....[18]

Family is clearly at the heart of it. But not just a human family, but a family born from above out of a radical revolution that linked us together in a life-flow from Christ himself: 'When I am raised to life again, you will know that I am in my Father, and you are in me, and I am in you.'[19] This essential relationship is described by Paul as us being a Body, joined to the Head – which by definition is totally interdependent, each part (however visible or not) being a living portion of the whole.

This family is in fact the family of God, or to take it further, the Godhead; Father, Son and Spirit that eternally co-exist in 'sweet community'.

> Even before he made the world, God loved us and chose us in Christ to be holy and without fault in his eyes. God decided in advance to adopt us into his own family by bringing us to himself through Jesus Christ.[20]

There is something so fundamental about this *relationship* based on the love and grace of the Trinity that intend us to be adopted, 'come

---

[18] Steve Botham, in social media discussion
[19] John 14:20 *Holy Bible*, New Living Translation, copyright © 1996, 2004, 2015 by Tyndale House Foundation.
[20] Ephesians 1:3-4 *Holy Bible*, New Living Translation, copyright © 1996, 2004, 2015 by Tyndale House Foundation.

of age' in this covenant bond together, that we should not diminish its importance.

Baxter Kruger describes this fundamental relationship so eloquently here:

> To believe in the Trinity means that we believe that God is a relational being, and always has been, and always will be. The doctrine of the Trinity means that relationship, that fellowship, that togetherness and sharing, that self-giving and other-centredness are not afterthoughts with God but the deepest truth about the being of God. The Father is not consumed with Himself; He loves the Son and the Spirit. And the Son is not riddled with narcissism; he loves his Father and the Spirit. And the Spirit is not preoccupied with himself and his own glory; the Spirit loves the Father and the Son. Giving, not taking; other centeredness, not self-centeredness; Sharing, not hoarding are what fire the rockets of God and lie at the very centre of God's existence as Father, Son and Spirit.

> When Christianity says God, it says relationship. It says self-giving love expressing itself in boundless fellowship and joyous and untold unity. It does not say self-centred. It does not say removed, distant, detached, indifferent or austere. It does not say lonely or sad or bored or in need. When Christianity says God, it says Father, Son and Spirit existing in a relationship of acceptance and delight and self-giving love, a relationship that is so true, so rich and real and good, so open that the only way we can speak of it is to say that God is three, yet utterly one. For while the Father, Son and Spirit remain eternally distinct, their love for one another is so pure

and their fellowship is so deep that any descriptive word short of "one" betrays the sheer reality of their togetherness.[21]

This beautiful life of the Trinity is ours in Jesus and we are being led by the Spirit to embody and express its fulness and glory in this life; this is the Truth of our Being. We just need to align the Way of our Being.[22] So whatever our expressions of *ekklesia* look like, whenever people touch us, they should encounter the Godhead in this way.

We live in a Western culture that has become incredibly individualistic, to a level that would be unknown in the ancient world (and is even rare in indigenous cultures today).

> Individualism. Narcissism. Value-free choices. These are all key elements in the decline of the practice of mutual accountability in Western churches, among clergy and laity alike.[23]

But as Francois du Toit renders 1Cor 12:19, 'Our individual significance only finds context in relationship to others!'[24] While each person is known by God and able to relate to the Godhead personally in Christ, the vast emphasis of the scriptures is plural, spoken to a gathered, related Body. Thus, Jesus tells us pray '*Our* Father', Peter refers to us a living stones joined in the corporate house of God, Paul refers to us together as the fully functioning Body of Christ.

---

[21] Dr Baxter Kruger, *Jesus and the Undoing of Adam* 2003 Perichoresis Press
[22] To borrow from George Macdonald's phrase.
[23] David Augsburger, American Anabaptist author
[24] Mirror Bible (paraphrase by Francois du Toit)

The words 'one another' appear about 100 times in statements in the New Testament, which can be seen perhaps to be not so much as imperatives as descriptive of the essential bond we now have in Christ. We are in a real sense "members of one another" (Romans 12:5; Ephesians 4:25).

So, love, acceptance, kindness …. all the fruit of the Spirit reveal the source of Life within our 'awakened communities of faith', outworked in a plethora of expressions like hospitality, shared meals, care for the vulnerable, practical love in action.

However, these things are not only seen in churches. Wherever we see these expressions of love we can recognise that Father, Son and Spirit are at work in human lives, and celebrate it. Thus, we can see Christ in everyone (even if they can't see it themselves). We can hold the same attitude to all. Hence Jesus says in Matthew 25:40 'Don't you know? When you cared for one of the least of these, my little ones, my true brothers and sisters, you demonstrated love for me.' Mother Theresa used to ask her sisters, 'Did you meet Jesus today?' when they cared for the destitute on the streets of Calcutta. So, while the *ekklesia* is essentially family, it is in no way meant to be in hermetically sealed containers, but porous, outward-looking communities that reflect the Christ who 'ate and drank with sinners.'

Clearly the church has morphed over the centuries as it has embraced a theology of separation, from God and from mankind. This has developed a sense that people are either 'in' or 'out', accepted or not, saved or lost. But perhaps the Lord never intended us to view others that way, instead seeing that all are held in Christ – in Adam all have died, so in Christ all are made alive – and the difference is between those who are awakened (through conversion) and those who are still asleep, unaware that it is now day? After all, we were only lost because we first belonged.

There has never been a time when loneliness has been felt more acutely than in the Covid-19 pandemic. Noreena Hertz in her book The Lonely Century[25], highlights the loss of community over recent decades – including churches – stressing that in a world of smart phones, economic growth and urbanisation, people feel more disconnected than ever. Hertz comments 'the infrastructure of community – by which I mean those shared spaces by which people of all stripes can come together, interact and form bonds – has been severely neglected at best and at worst actively destroyed.' This is a fundamental part of our calling as *ekklesia* – to provide a place of belonging for 'all stripes' i.e., not just the preferred group of friends who agree with us, but the breadth of society. 'We're living in an age when we have forgotten a fundamental truth about humankind that is as old as the Hebrew Bible itself: that we were not meant to live alone.'[26]

The development of online live streaming, with Zoom and other platforms, has opened many new possibilities for connection. It enabled people to link in or interact regardless of geography or other restrictions. There are many benefits, and it can be a great adjunct to *ekklesia*. However, we must also be clear about the limitations of 'virtual church'. If the incarnation shows us anything, it is that physical connection is fundamental to who we are now in Christ. We all need 'love with flesh on' – people to touch, to hug, to feed and be fed by, to share with in the ups and downs of life. We miss so many of the

---

[25] Noreena Hertz, The Lonely Century, Sceptre Books 2020
[26] Endorsement to The Lonely Century, 2020, by Rabbi Lord Jonathan Sachs

subtle signs, the nuances of meaning, the awareness of 'atmosphere' when we are only relating through a screen.

Brian Zahnd is fairly outspoken about this; 'To prefer digital over enfleshed is a gnostic move; it's a move away from what it means to be human; it's an insult to the Incarnation…. When we "gather" online we mostly just watch something, and we can entirely control the experience. If we choose, we can just lurk and leave whenever we like. That may seem preferable, but it's not church. Church throws us into the company of people who, left to our own devices, we would probably never have any interaction with. But these are precisely the people we need to meet, get to know, and learn to love. Left to our own (electronic) devices we will be stunted in our Christian maturity. For God so loved the world that he didn't send a text message — he sent his Son in person.'[27] As the old adage says, you can choose your friends, but you can't choose your family. We are born into it.

Christianity is sacramental, taking water, oil, bread and wine, laying on of hands and holy embrace; virtual church can never replace physical connection. The shared sacraments are very important: 'there seems to me to be a way in which … the church is an indispensable conduit of the fulness of God's grace being meditated to us.'[28] The early church clearly gathered in loving communities, extended families, recognisable groups. They ate together, 'broke bread', taught, encouraged, loved, helped, worshipped together. As an awakened family, they were a living prophetic sign of God's love in their society 'so that through the church the manifold wisdom of God might now be made known to the rulers and authorities in the

---

[27] Brian Zahnd (Word of Life Church, Missouri) Facebook post 2020
[28] Paul Golf, in an email discussion 2021.

heavenly places'[29] or as the Mirror Bible said it, 'The ekklesia disperses the varied magnitude of God like a prism, in human form.'[30] If our churches, of whatever form or size, do not have this sort of **family** at the very heart, then we surely need a rethink. The scale we connect through needs to be small enough so it can take place in a home, a café, a canteen or wherever that allows for genuine relationships to flourish, regardless of how it may fit into a larger structure.

What other things are key?

Jesus clearly loved gatherings, meals, parties …. in fact, his critics homed in on him for 'eating and drinking' with who they considered the wrong kind of people. In fact, **food** has been an integral aspect of our faith since the days of the patriarchs, as God sealed covenants – in accordance with Middle Eastern tradition – over a meal. To the Orthodox Jew, Sabbath still begins in the evening with a Shabbat meal, after which they go and sleep – surely a good picture of the 'rest' that we are now to live in.

In the upper room, Jesus gave us his New [renewed] Covenant in the context of a Passover meal with the twelve, emphasising the centrality of our participation through simple bread and wine.

> Your every meal makes the mandate of his coming relevant and communicates the meaning of the New Covenant.[31]

---

[29] Ephesians 3:10 ESV
[30] Ephesians 3:10b Mirror Bible (paraphrase by Francois du Toit)
[31] 1 Corinthians 11:26 Mirror Bible (paraphrase by Francois du Toit)

It is clear that the early church laid great importance on this following his ascension.

Throughout the centuries, the church has made this communion meal a central aspect of our expression of faith. Sometimes this has become very formal and liturgical, at other times very simple and intimate. At the time of the sixteenth century Scottish Reformation, the cavernous High Kirk of St Giles in Edinburgh was subdivided into four, because they believed that a church should not be larger than the number that could gather around a table, such value was placed on this shared meal.

Eating food together is such a perfect way to deepen relationship. It forces us to slow down – in fact if we can prepare food together, all the better – and the unhurried nature of a meal allows for sharing of hearts in an informal, often light-hearted setting. We can so easily include others in a meal, showing we value them and offer friendship. Conversations develop naturally when cooking and clearing up. It is not all we are about, but as we reimagine *ekklesia*, it is a great starting place.

There are of course traditional aspects of church life that have been handed down through the generations which will continue in some form or another, but these are all also subject to re-imagining: worship, prophecy, teaching, leadership, discipleship and evangelism. Many of these have become rather stereotyped over the years – we need to consider their **relevance** in the 21st century. The *ekklesia* was not intended to form an alternative ghetto, a subculture that was undecipherable to those who were not in the know. Rather we were called to serve humanity with the values of Jesus and to prepare it to receive his now-coming Kingdom.

This is not to say that we ignore the lessons of previous generations. As mentioned, the Celtic church in the British Isles in the 5th - 8th centuries AD gave us a rich example of an engaged Christian community displaying love and care as they spread good news. Despite the influx of pagan Anglo-Saxon tribes into southern and eastern Britain, the Celts were not overwhelmed but instead spread the Christian gospel throughout. Based more on relationship around a monastic tradition rather than being organised into parishes, Celtic spirituality showed us examples of hospitality, friendship and the holistic care of all of creation, undergirded by a firm Trinitarian theology. There were many reports of healings and miracles and, although these accounts may be dismissed by liberals today, they point to a rich heritage of 'encounter' with God. While not perfect, the Celtic church was certainly effective enough to turn druids around and cause pagan incomers to covert to Christ.

We can learn from the Celtic appreciation of the natural world. For example, the climate crisis is headline news in our world just now. The *ekklesia* can show her relevance by leading in this discussion rather than dismissing it, or burying her head in the sand (assuming, with twisted theology, that we will all exit the planet and leave the rest to get on with it). Genesis 1 and 2 convey to us the truth that God created all things, including man in his image. Therefore, man (Adam, literally 'likeness-made-from-soil'[32]) is to rule in the same manner as God does, with love and compassion, not indifference and detached domination. Young people are understandably angry and frustrated at older generations for the pollution and exploitation of the planet – this is an area that we should speak to with hope and clarity, leading the way in making a difference.

---

[32] Francois du Toit

Teaching is clearly important in the Christian tradition: the 'faith handed down' (the importance of this is developed further in a subsequent chapter). However, we are in a different day now in which most people are not used to long sermons or wading through hefty study volumes. We may regret this, but the technological developments of recent decades have given humans a shorter attention span. Nevertheless, there are good aspects too; the growth of independent learning, the widening of resources available (on the Internet), the development of mind mapping and other forms of thinking 'out of the box'. Yet some of our churches have been accused of indoctrination – at their worst, even forming cult status – and insecure leaders have sometimes been resistant to question or challenge. We need to recognise that people need a **voice** today: we should listen to our congregations and recognise that it is together that we have the mind of Christ. Yes, we can honour those who are called to lead and have studied in depth, but we should not place them on pedestals. We should rather recognise that each person has the Spirit of God living in them (including the children). We can raise a voice for justice, defending those who have lost their voice.

Styles of leadership are worth considering. It is an over-generalisation, but often leadership in traditional churches seems to be characterised by qualities of humility, learning and spirituality. In new or charismatic churches, leaders are often visionary, pioneering A-type personalities (understandably, as they have often broken new ground away from the apparent constriction of the old). One observation, though, is that the new churches have found it less easy to pass on leadership from one generation to another and 'founding leaders' often find it difficult to let go of control. This can lead to pyramidical structures that at best can feel domineering and at worst can be open to abuse or division. As we reconsider *ekklesia*, maybe our communities should have the qualities of leadership that undergird and release – more like an inverted pyramid – yes, visionary and capable yet releasing and empowering at the same time. Discipleship can thrive more naturally in healthy, relational settings.

Worship is something that we see throughout the scriptures, particularly in the Psalms and in the Book of Revelation. The apostle Paul encouraged us to 'sing psalms, hymns and spiritual songs' when we come together. However, in many contemporary churches this has now equated to what one young observer described recently as 'American soft rock'. That may be accessible but has become hackneyed and predictable.

The church is the embodiment of creativity with Christ as the head, so all forms of worship should flourish; art, dance, rhythm, poetry, song, in fact all of life. Indigenous forms of worship should be celebrated rather than despised. Martin Neil is a leading drummer who has sat with native American tribes, valuing their gifts and encouraging them to express their praise and worship in their own culture. Voices from the Nations[33] aims to celebrate music from around the world, encouraging its incredible diversity and discovering the stories that help us understand their unique melodies and sounds. The *ekklesia* can demonstrate this creativity at every level.

One encouraging development is to see how the different streams of spirituality are flowing together more in these days. So, the sacramental, the liturgical, the contemplative cross-pollinate with the livelier charismatic, colourful and creative expressions. Many

---

[33] Martin and Rebekah Neil are musical wanderers who have a passion for creativity and storytelling. Visit www.voicesfromthenations.org to find out more.

communities are enjoying exploring new forms, embracing contemplative practices, Lectio Divina, stillness and the like. When we acknowledge that there is still mystery in the wonder of our faith – even though Christ is 'the mystery revealed' – it allows us to explore the vastness of our mystical union with him. It has been said, 'the Christian of the future will be a mystic, or will not exist.'[34] There is a great search for peace in this hurried, stressed-out world. We can demonstrate the beauty of this mystery, as we abide in the Prince of Peace.

We have been guilty of suggesting sometimes that worship is only what takes place in meetings or services. Paul teaches in Romans 12 that our whole lives are acts of worship though. Some people who are called to the business realm, to caring professions, to innovation and science or to academia can feel like a 'fish out of water' in a traditional worship setting. We need to help them see that what they do is equally an act of worship and go out of our way to value each and every person in their God-given attributes and gifts – after all, the Trinity expresses their glory through our lives in a myriad of different ways. False dualisms, separating sacred and secular, alienate those we seek to serve.

Because the *ekklesia* is the embodiment of Christ, power and Presence are already given to us. Yet many of our songs and prayers are us asking God to give us what he has already provided us in Christ! We adopt an Old Testament attitude of having to progress through the temple courts, or climb the mountain, without realising that in Christ we are *already* in the Holy Place. The issue is not that we have to ask God to come, rather that we need to awaken to the reality that

---

[34] Karl Rahner (1904 – 1984), a German Jesuit priest and theologian

he *has* come and lives in us: we are united with him! The church should be a place of **encounter** above all else.

It was not his great learning and theology that brought Saul to Christ, it was his encounter on the road to Damascus. Metropolitan Anthony describes how as a young man, raised in Russia and Iran, he was well-schooled in communist, atheistic thought, yet when someone gave him the Gospel of Mark he experienced an encounter that answered his questions and reorientated his worldview in an instant.[35] Encounter made the difference.

We so often expect people to come to us, to our meetings, to our events when they are busy getting on with their, albeit broken, lives. We need to be in and out among society, offering encounter in daily life, expecting God to display life-changing healing and wholeness through us. All this is in the context of good news, as we share about a Saviour who has come to us before we ever thought of him.

> The church... is in the Gospel-proclaiming business. It is not here to bring the world the bad news that God will think kindly about us only after we have gone through certain creedal, liturgical and ethical wickets; it is here to bring the world the Good News that 'while we were yet sinners, Christ died for the ungodly.' It is here, in short, for no religious purpose at all, only to announce the Gospel of free grace.[36]

---

[35] Metropolitan Anthony of Sourozh, School for Prayer, Darton, Longman & Todd Ltd 1999. He rose to become the he ad of the Russian Orthodox Church in Britain.
[36] Robert Farrar Capon, Kingdom, Grace, Judgment, Eerdmans 1985

To read media accounts of the church, it would be easy to see that we have so often been guilty of 'ungrace'[37], rather than coming as Christ did, to hurting, broken people. If we are to be relevant in this age, people that meet us should be able to taste the unrelenting, amazing grace of a Father who has always loved them. They need to feel his welcome through us before their lives are sorted out, their issues resolved. We can speak to the treasure within as we 'gossip the gospel of grace' in our daily lives.

So what might a new ecclesiology look like?

I have been careful not to describe the externals of what *ekklesia* should look like, or how it should be organised, as this depends entirely on context and should be led by the Spirit. Yet, the values and essence of a new ecclesiology are clearly apparent.

Church must however be **authentic**. This generation wants something real and engaging, avoiding any hint of window dressing or hypocrisy. Jesus spoke of us as salt in society – salt changes the taste of everything – and spoke of us as light – he shines through us in a dark world.

> We should not be viewing anyone according to the flesh – appearance/race/intelligence/sexuality/connections – but make room for the authenticity of the other person, taking them seriously, listening, whether we agree or not. The church – in people – should be the living embodiment of the Trinity on earth.

---

[37] Philip Yancey's expression in 'What's so amazing about Grace', Zondervan 2002

Ask people in church, "what are your passions, what fires your rockets, what are your dreams, what is your deepest joy, what do you most enjoy...?"[38]

It is this level of reality, of engaging with one another in the joys and sorrows of everyday life, that is key.

A recent radio interview gave an account of a pastor in the States showing his son the great facilities his church had, the library, the gymnasium, the extensive campus and saying to him, 'one day this will all be yours!' But his son, who was studying at college, said to him 'Dad, I don't want any of this! I just want to get together with my friends, have some beers, maybe crack open a Bible and talk about the things that really matter to us.' It was not that the father was necessarily wrong, it just illustrated that it was not what his son's generation were looking for. And they are leaving the former, corporate style of church in great numbers.

This generation is not giving up on spirituality, it is just looking for it in other places.

> Young adults are satisfied leaving church because they are redefining religion on their own terms. Millennials start making their worldly lives into their religions, they turn meditation into their search for spirituality, they visit gyms like they're synagogues and they turn to therapists in exchange for prayer. This generation has not chosen to

---

[38] Dr Baxter Kruger, Conference at Wellsprings Community, Edinburgh 2015

abandon religion, just to look for it in everything else they do.[39]

As believers, we see that these young adults are 'scratching the itch' but not addressing the core issue, that the Lover of our souls, the One who holds all things together, is the only one who can truly heal the human condition. Only the Light of the World can illumine the darkness in our minds. And he has a Body of awakened people – a family – through which he shares this good news.

We must all own our influences and history in this discussion. I am an architect by profession but have the role as pastor/leader of our small, creative church called Wellsprings Community (who give me some regular financial support). I don't call myself 'pastor', seeing this as a function rather than a title. I have had experience of the Anglican Church, the Church of Scotland, the Pentecostal church, the house churches – and also of a painful church split twenty years ago – but generally my story has been positive. Yet I acknowledge others have suffered misunderstanding, criticism or outright abuse in their experience of church, and this understandably colours their view. But somehow, when reconsidering *ekklesia* for the 21st Century, we need to avoid cynicism and overthinking; our faith is, after all, based on simple, childlike trust. If we focus on our intimacy with Jesus, living 'present' in the Holy Spirit, aware of our inclusion through Christ in the Godhead, then we can see *ekklesia* for who she is meant to be, the Bride in harmony with the Groom. In maturity we can be honest about the mistakes or faults that have been made, but also have grace for those that have failed along the way. Most are well intentioned,

---

[39] Christian Smith, a sociology and religion professor at the University of Notre Dame, USA 2021

even if sometimes misguided. Brad Jersak's 'godfather' in the Eastern Orthodox Church, David Goa, comments on how vitriolic the attack on institutional church can become and adds:

> Unfortunately, the [anti-institutional church] crowd can be very puritanical. Why? Because their "pure" sense of things actually means "my personal pure notion is enough for me." But is it?

> The truth is that our self-understanding is *all* based in relationships or the lack thereof. Yes, the victims of religion may need to leave for a time of detox. But their victimization may also become their identity and if so, they will create a script that you must sign onto or you have no voice.[40]

We always need to guard against overreaction. The answer for the church today is not to try to compete with ever more fancy programmes, use techno wizardry or embrace woke philosophies. The *ekklesia* exists to **authentically** display Jesus Christ to a needy and hurting world, offering the love of a warm **family**, clear **relevance**, a listened-to **voice** and a genuine **encounter** with the Godhead today. We still need the gathered church in our neighbourhoods. This can come in many sizes and shapes, but sometimes small communities can adapt more easily where large find it hard to change. These can best be organic, creative, participatory, free – non-religious in culture while drawing on the heritage of the saints – sharing the *really* good news, expressing life in it fulness, displaying true love, joy and peace in the very heart of humankind.

---

[40] An article in the online Clarion Journal – see www.clarion-journal.com

In the second section, I develop further some of the distinctives of *ekklesia* and in the third section, consider three case studies of how some contemporary, grace-orientated churches have been seeking to express this.

The appendix includes some of the simple worship formats we have developed as contributions to our community life: a series of simple contemporary liturgies or offices written or adapted by Wellsprings Community and used alongside free worship in our regular communion times.

The series Monday-Friday was originally developed for use together on Zoom, at midday, during the Covid pandemic lockdown.

i.	Morning Office
ii.	Evening Office
iii.	Monday
iv.	Tuesday
v.	Wednesday
vi.	Thursday
vii.	Friday
viii.	Communion with the Wild Trinity

TWO | COMMUNITY

As has already been mentioned in reference to family, a sense of belonging or 'community' is something this age is crying out for. The individualism of the Western societies has become endemic, and the resultant mental, health related issues are well known. Many homes are broken through family strife or just by people moving away. God has something different in mind for humanity!

The church has not been immune from controversy and harm in this area. Yet that is not a reason to reject *ekklesia*, rather a spur for reformation. Our starting place for understanding what God had in mind is the Holy Trinity, and the Person of Christ revealed in human flesh.

As stated in the first chapter, the Godhead *is* present before anything else, dwelling in perfect harmony and 'sweet community'. While the term Trinity may not appear in the scriptures, what it describes of a God-in-three-persons is clearly proclaimed. We see in Genesis 1 that God says, 'Let us make man in our image' and in Abraham's three visitors we have a foreshadowing of the Trinity. In many places in the New Testament the essential relationship between the Three Persons of one God is evident; at Jesus' baptism, the Son gets wet, the Father speaks, and the Spirit descends like a dove; in the upper room Jesus tells Philip, 'If you have seen me you have seen the Father' and then promises in the sending of the Spirit, in effect 'another like me.'

The amazing revelation we are given in the New Testament is that the Godhead, dwelling in a circle of perfect love, chose to widen that before time began to include us also.

> For he chose us in him before the creation of the world to be holy and blameless in his sight.[41]

The concept of the Trinity is hard for us to grasp; it's not surprising that some strange ideas have emerged! Yet it retains an aspect of mystery; something we should not be afraid of but embrace with faith. Three persons, yet one essence (*homoousious*[42]) as the early Church Fathers established when forming the Nicene Creed. Different in role but not hierarchical; each Person equally God, yet distinct. Thus, Jesus is fully God and fully man, and therefore is able to fully heal mankind of the disease of sin, entering into our darkness and dross, and redeeming us 'from the inside'.

There has been a trend to suggest that the deity of Christ was just a fourth century construct at the behest of the emperor Constantine. However, this is patently untrue. As well as the scriptural and Apostolic witness to the Lordship of Christ, the Church Fathers (such as Polycarp, Gregory, Irenaeus) all consistently taught this – often at the cost of their own lives. It was only promulgation of the Arian heresy[43] that prompted Athanasius and the early bishops to clarify the relationship and nature of the Trinity – and the resultant Nicene Creed is now an indispensable aid to our understanding.

---

[41] Eph 1:4 New International Version®, NIV® Copyright ©1973, 1978, 1984, 2011 by Biblica, Inc.®

[42] A theological term 'same in being, same in essence', from ὁμός, *homós*, "same" and οὐσία, *ousía*, "being" or "essence" clarifying the ontology of Christ

[43] Arius was a Christian presbyter from Alexandria, Egypt AD 256-336 who denied that Jesus existed before birth, and thus was not co-eternal with the Father.

At the heart of the Creed is the description of *relationship*; it is this that is at the core of all God intends for us, to also lead healthy and wholesome lives. In other words, lives that display the Kingdom of God.

Paul describes the Kingdom as:

> Righteous, peace and joy…..in the Holy Spirit.[44]

When we consider *ekklesia*, we should not start with forms, patterns, definitions, dogma – rather we should start with Jesus Christ. Paul's letter to the Colossians teaches that all things are created through him and held in place by his word of power. We are made new and exist 'in Christ':

> For you have acquired new creation life which is continually being renewed into the likeness of the One who created you, giving you the full revelation of God.[45]

Paul goes on to explain in the next line how in this new community, former demarcations or divisions are erased:

> In this new creation life, your nationality makes no difference, nor your ethnicity, education, nor economic status–they matter nothing. For it is Christ that means everything as he lives in every one of us.[46]

---

[44] Rom 14:17 New International Version®, NIV® Copyright ©1973, 1978, 1984, 2011 by Biblica, Inc.®

[45] Col 3:10 The Passion Translation®. Copyright © 2017, 2018, 2020 by Passion & Fire Ministries, Inc.

[46] Col 3:11 The Passion Translation®. Copyright © 2017, 2018, 2020 by Passion & Fire Ministries, Inc.

This is so exciting: a total fresh start! Our gathered groups can reflect a bond that transcends any disputes over gender, race or political emphasis. As Francois du Toit paraphrases it in the Mirror:

> The revelation of Christ in us gives identity to the individual beyond anything anyone could ever be as a Greek or a Jew, American or African, foreigner or famous, male or female, king or pawn. From now on everyone is defined by Christ; everyone is represented in Christ.[47]

So as Baxter Kruger says, 'in the end the whole discussion of what is church is really a footnote to 'who is Jesus?''

Of course, the Father, Son and Holy Spirit are at work everywhere, so whenever we see other-giving love and kindness we can acknowledge and appreciate this. We are not to assume the moral high-ground and look down on others – this has so often led to accusations of hypocrisy and arrogance – but rather as those who have awakened to the Gospel, we can proclaim this wholeheartedly in our connecting together! We have something so good to celebrate.

Part of our role as the Body of Christ is to incarnate the truths of the Gospel in our everyday lives. We need one another to do this. We are 'hardwired' for love and encouragement; this is a key aspect of the need to gather. I have seen on so many occasions that when people move to the periphery – perhaps though over-busyness or having taken some offence through the actions of others – then only a while later they are struggling and seem to give up on the faith they once knew.

---

[47] Col 3:11 Mirror Bible (paraphrase by Francois du Toit)

Some people can cope with isolation and may even seek this for a more contemplative lifestyle, away from the distraction and stress of contemporary life. The Desert Fathers and Mothers were probably of this ilk. Yet apparently even many of them used to leave their caves or refuges and gather with others on Sundays to celebrate the Eucharist, and actually had considerable contact with visitors or local villagers.[48]

Most of us need one another to remind each other of our identity. Luther apparently said that we need to hear the Gospel every day! What I think he was addressing is our tendency, as human beings, to let the pressing need of the moment fill our minds. Discouragement or disillusionment may come if challenges abound. Feelings can be so unreliable. Jesus referred to the Devil as the Accuser, who 'has been a liar from the start.' Having been defeated at the cross, the enemy – however we may interpret him – has only one real card: that of illusion, deceit and threat through 'smoke and mirrors'. The defeated, servile, law-bound mindset he represents can still try to capture those who have enjoyed freedom – hence the sharp warnings in the Book of Hebrews not to revert to a D-I-Y, legalistic approach.

Paul encourages the Corinthian church (as recorded in 1 Cor 10), before going on to explain the significance of their fellowship meals together:

> v13 Your situation is not unique. Every human life faces contradictions. Here is the Good news: God believes in your

---

[48] The Lives of the Desert Fathers: Introduction by Benedicta Ward SLG p.26ff, published by Mowbray 1980

freedom. He has made it possible for you to triumph in every situation that you will ever encounter.

v17   The single loaf of bread that we all partake of represents the fact that although there are many of us, there is only one Christ. By eating together from that one bread we are declaring that we are one body in Christ and that he is incarnated in each one of us. (Our "many-ness" becomes "one-ness;" Christ doesn't become fragmented in us. Rather, we become unified in him. — The Message)[49]

We encourage one another to remember the work Christ completed for us and that we are all part of that one new man, that corporate new creation.

But encourage one another daily, as long as it is called "Today", so that none of you may be hardened by sin's deceitfulness.[50]

Instead, remind yourselves daily of your true identity; make today count. Do not allow callousness of heart to cheat any of you for even a single day out of your allotted portion.[51]

We all have a need to experience that love. We can do that to some extent online and via social media, but we will need to gather in person to experience 'love with skin on'.

---

[49] Mirror Bible (paraphrase by Francois du Toit)
[50] Heb 3:13 New International Version®, NIV® Copyright ©1973, 1978, 1984, 2011 by Biblica, Inc.®
[51] Heb 3:13 Mirror Bible (paraphrase by Francois du Toit)

Physical connection with people that we can hug or share our homes and meal tables with is vital. Of course, some are more comfortable with close contact than others – cultural differences may influence us here – but many wellness experts have emphasised how with physical touch our quality-of-life improves. We are not alone in this, but this is one area that the *ekklesia* makes a difference.

THREE | SACRAMENT

The *ekklesia* has a particular role given to her by the Lord at the Last Supper: that of sharing this New Covenant meal in our gatherings. While of course it can be taken alone, the context is clearly that of the community.

> And he took bread, gave thanks and broke it, and gave it to them, saying, "This is my body given for you; do this in remembrance of me."
> In the same way, after the supper he took the cup, saying, "This cup is the new covenant in my blood, which is poured out for you...."[52]

Remembrance has particular connotations here. It could be translated 'recollection': Jesus is doing more than saying 'remember I was here with you' as with a photo on the mantlepiece, he is saying in effect 'be continually mindful of what I have done for you – becoming flesh, dying, rising and ascending – not as an example for you, but as an example of you.'[53] The church community has had a particular role in stewarding this, down through the centuries. Yet, it is to be seen as far more than a memorial meal: it is a declaration now of the present, abiding outcome of the full and sufficient work of the Son of God for humanity. Francois du Toit comments on this verse:

---

[52] Luke 22: 19-20 New International Version®, NIV® Copyright ©1973, 1978, 1984, 2011 by Biblica, Inc.®
[53] T.F Torrance and Dr Baxter Kruger are among those who stress the entirety of the work of Christ

> Make your meals a continual celebration of your incarnation mirrored in me (Present Active Imperative ποιειτε *poiete*, continue to do by repetition).[54]

We call this meal Communion. The Latin root of communion is *communionem*, meaning **"fellowship, mutual participation, or sharing**." The amazing truth borne out in the Gospel is that we participate in the life of the Godhead through Christ, and as the Apostle Paul repeatedly emphasises, we are now 'in Christ', no longer as independent agents but sharing together in the Life of the Ages. While this is a work for all – Jesus is Saviour of the World – it is something that those who have awakened/been converted celebrate regularly, reminding themselves of who they really are now! (How sad that over the centuries some traditions have sought to bar others from participating in this meal, for fear of judgement.)

Other traditions refer to this communion meal as the eucharist, which derives from the thanksgiving Jesus gave at the outset of this meal. It contains within it the word *'charis'* (grace) – we could see that as expressing thanks for the grace of God. Some may also refer to this as the Mass, or simply the Breaking of Bread.

Above all, this meal is seen as a **sacrament**: a visible, tangible representation of the grace of God. The word sacrament comes from a Latin version of the Greek root meaning 'Mystery'.[55] Along with the other sacraments, baptism, anointing with oil – the Catholics identify

---

[54] Luke 22:19 Mirror Bible (paraphrase by Francois du Toit)
[55] Ref. John Crowder's three-part series on Sacrament. Apparently Middle English: from Old French *sacrement*, from Latin *sacramentum* 'solemn oath' (from *sacrare* 'to hallow', from *sacer* 'sacred'), used in Christian Latin as a translation of Greek *mustērion* 'mystery'

seven[56] – there is a sense in which these have been entrusted to the *ekklesia* to value and pass on down through the generations. We don't need to see this in an exclusive sense, rather a wonderful privilege to share with any who are willing to embrace God's love.

We don't 'make anything happen' when we take Communion together, or when we baptise someone, rather we declare what has happened in Christ!

> [Christ is] our High Priest who by his vicarious atoning sacrifice for our sins, cleanses us and sanctifies us so that he may lead us into the holy presence of the Father – the Holy of Holies – this is how we must understand both Baptism and the Lord's Supper through which we participate in what he has done for us, once and for all, and is continuing to do....[57]

There is a sense in which we affirm how precious these things are when we come together and do them in community: they are not just trifles that we take or leave on a whim. Yet we may certainly throw off the religious practices or expectations that have been laid on us in relation to this. Communion does not need to be a solemn affair; yes, it recognises the ultimate act of the Lord laying down his life for us, but 'it was for the joy set before him that he endured the cross.' Jesus wants us to live in that joy! I love the way the New Mystics[58] celebrate the sharing of bread and wine like a party. Perhaps the rest of the world would not see us as sober-minded, dour-faced religionists if we

---

[56] Baptism, Confirmation, Eucharist, Reconciliation, Anointing of the Sick, Matrimony, and Holy Orders

[57] J.B.Torrance 'Worship, Community and the Triune God of Grace' Paternoster Press 1996

[58] John Crowder and friends at Sons of Thunder; see https://www.thenewmystics.com/

learned to let our hair down and actually enjoy celebrating the Gospel!

> When faith in Christ's act of love becomes your solid foundation, then you have a dance floor that can handle your joy. Wave after wave of glorious bliss flows from this unwavering union, sealed with blood. Life becomes an unending expression of the divine, because experience is no longer based on your efforts but his.[59]

There is another sacrament my friend Colin Symes refers to, the **sacrament of encounter**. In this he discusses the work of Martin Buber, who taught on 'I - Thou' being a relationship of mutuality and reciprocity, while 'I - It' being a relationship of separateness and detachment[60]. Buber initially developed these ideas about how we relate to God, but they also apply to how we encounter one another. We acutely need one another to help mature one another in who we already are in Christ.

There is a dimension of oneness in our mystical union that is so profound, we encounter Christ in our midst:

> For wherever two or three come together in honour of my name, I am right there with them! (Matt 18:20 TPT)

In Rublev's extraordinary ikon of the Trinity, one can see something of this connection between each person as they gaze at one another.

---

[59] John Crowder 'Mystical Union' p196 Sons of Thunder Ministries and Publications
[60] Martin Buber (1878-1965) was a German philosopher who's most notable work was Ich und Du (1923; I and Thou)

Colin speaks of how that dynamic that is going on in the Trinity can go on through us. He shares a story of how after a training course the leaders came to say goodbye to the group, but instead of saying anything they just stopped at each person and looked intently, loving each one with their eyes. Almost all were in tears because there was a connection, an encounter that they embodied.

The *ekklesia* has something precious to offer through sacrament, entrusted to her by the Lord, that when tired, fearful, hungry, dispirited humanity discover it, they will embrace it with joy and relief.

FOUR | WELLBEING

There is another dimension to *ekklesia* that we can explore which is to do with integrity, which I've put under the heading of the health or wellbeing of the message. It is common today for people to question whether there is such a thing as absolute truth. Yet we would understand that ultimately truth is a Person, Jesus Christ, not an idea or a statement of belief or a collection of religious doctrines. Nevertheless, though we should be free from pedantic arguments over precise wording of proof texts, or cul-du-sacs such as the 'inerrancy of scripture'[61], we still use words as well as actions to pass on the Good News.

It has been noted by some that there is a difference between tradition and traditionalism (in this context) – the former identifies what is precious and how it is handed on through the generations, while the latter tends to refer to narrow religiosity. The Apostle Paul emphasised to Timothy:

> '...the things you have heard me say in the presence of many witnesses entrust to reliable people who will also be qualified to teach others.'[62]

There was something here about the importance of the passing on what was the clear revelation of the Gospel, treasured, entrusted,

---

[61] Brad Jersak deals with this modernist view very effectively in his book 'A More Christlike Word', published by Whitaker House 2021
[62] 2 Tim 2:2 New International Version®, NIV® Copyright ©1973, 1978, 1984, 2011 by Biblica, Inc.®

precious, the tradition you could say of the reliable teaching about the incarnation, death, resurrection and ascension of the Son of God, and our wonderful inclusion in him.

> The church is vital because it's familiar with something that others are not experiencing, and it is Life.[63]

As has been mentioned, the Nicene Creed affirmed 'the holy catholic and apostolic church' in recognition that it was not just the written witness that speaks of Jesus Christ, but the shared experience of the encounter with him that is passed down through the ages.

If our Christology is weak, we will be vulnerable to adding to the simplicity of the Good News our man-made ideas about the things that we consider necessary to 'be a Christian'. Being Christ-centred may be good, but even that does not go far enough. We can subtly add systems, requirements, do-this, do-that, try harder to follow this way of the Master. However, the language of the Gospel is not DO, but DONE. The message of Hebrews could be summed up that we have left "Self-effortania' and entered "Grace-land" – we are now invited to cease from our labours and to promptly enter the rest that is Christ. He *is* our Promised Land, our eternal Sabbath rest!

All sorts of aberrations can develop if this is not understood.

It is delightful to see that many who were stuck on a treadmill of 'work harder', 'try to be a better Christian' – always seeing their relationship with God as a sort of Snakes and Ladders game, in which some days you are climbing closer to him only to slip up and slide back down

---

[63] Baxter Kruger in a zoom conversation on this subject, November 2022.

again – now discovering a freedom and assurance that it was Christ's finished work on the cross that achieved all that was necessary. Acceptance and adoption are at the core of the Good News.

Yet some who were prominent in sharing what they consider a 'Grace-message'– and revelling in the freedom it brings – have then slid away from an essential dependence on Christ to a generalised, mystical spirituality. This is more New Age than New Testament. The wonder at God's goodness expressed through humanity and creation, and of us being released from a fearful observance of a distant God, is of no lasting benefit if we gradually erase the uniqueness of Jesus from the picture. To some, he has become a spaceman, to others some eternal cosmic energy! They are led by the latest YouTube pop-philosophy or conspiracy theory into some new spiritual construct or other – which is in reality no more than sliding back into a form of religion dressed in a new suit. As if we could go *beyond* the revelation of God's only Son!

This sort of challenge was not absent from the early church. In fact, the writer to the Hebrews has to spell it out in stark, First Century terms to the Jewish Christians who were sliding back to Judaism: "there is absolutely no other way than the one God has provided though his Son – don't give up on the free gift of Life – anything else is anathema!"

> Do not be swayed by distracting speculations. Any influence foreign to what grace communicates, even if it seems very entertaining and caries the Christian label, is to be shunned. Feast on grace; do not dilute your diet with legalism. There is

no nourishment left in the law. What's the use of being busy but not blessed? [64]

To guard against individual interpretations or the latest pseudo-revelation, God has placed us in his *ekklesia*, with a credal faith handed down from the Church Fathers. None of us has perfect theology - we are all on a journey of understanding this wonderful Gospel – but we have been given safeguards against the ditches either side of the road. Firstly, we have the scriptures which, while they need to be seen through the lens of Christ (as Jesus explained to the two travellers to Emmaus[65]), give faithful testimony to God's revelation of his Son. But secondly, we have the teaching handed down, which we understand as orthodox faith.

In the early centuries the Gospel was being challenged by the Gnostics, who struggled with the humanity of Christ, and the Arians, who could not accept his divinity. When the bishops, aided by the young Athanasius, gathered at Nicaea in AD 325 to compile the Nicene Creed (which was further developed in 381), they clarified these key issues:

> We believe in one God, the Father, the Almighty,
> maker of heaven and earth, of all that is seen and unseen.
> We believe in one Lord, Jesus Christ, the only Son of God,
> eternally begotten of the Father,

---

[64] Heb 13:9 Mirror Bible (paraphrase by Francois du Toit)
[65] As they walked to Emmaus (Luke 24:13-35), Jesus explained to them the meaning of all the scriptures concerning himself. When they arrived in Emmaus, Jesus "took bread, blessed and broke it, and gave it to them," and their eyes were opened

God from God, Light from Light,
true God from true God, begotten not made, one in being
with the Father.
Through him all things were made.
For us and for our salvation he came down from heaven;
by the power of the Holy Spirit
he was born of the Virgin Mary, and became man.
For our sake he was crucified under Pontius Pilate,
he suffered, died, and was buried.
On the third day he rose again in fulfilment of the Scriptures;
he ascended into heaven and is seated at the right hand of
the Father.
He will come again in glory to judge the living and the dead,
and his kingdom will have no end.
We believe in the Holy Spirit, the Lord, the giver of life,
who proceeds from the Father and the Son.
With the Father and the Son he is worshipped and glorified.
He has spoken through the prophets.
We believe in one, holy, catholic, and apostolic Church.
We acknowledge one baptism for the forgiveness of sins.
We look for the resurrection of the dead,
and the life of the world to come.

This was particularly to address the rampant Arianism, but interestingly enough it does not focus so much on what Christ did as the relationship between the members of the Trinity. It affirms clearly that the Three-in-One were of 'one essence' (*homoousios* Gk), equal in status while distinct in role. This was not a new idea drummed up at the time, but the heart of the faith handed down.

This understanding of Jesus Christ becomes a litmus test. If our Christology fails here, then we soon veer off into confusion, or at best, ideas of our own making.

> For, there is one God and one Mediator who can reconcile God and humanity—the man Christ Jesus. [66]

Furthermore, we understand through Colossians that all things are formed through and by him and held by his word of power.

> For in him was created the universe of things, both in the heavenly realm and on the earth, all that is seen and all that is unseen. Every seat of power, realm of government, principality, and authority—it all exists through him and for his purpose![67]

Unfortunately, some speakers get 'put on a pedestal' by others, even if they don't seek it themselves. Respect is one thing, but adulation is unnecessary and unhelpful for anyone. The nature of God is humility – if his saints are not displaying that, one may wonder what they are aligning with. Others start to peddle their version of the truth. They can become lone interpreters, influencers who cause much damage. Very often, when this happens, it is apparent that they are not really answerable to anyone (except, they may say, 'God told me' or some similar statement). There is no one who can 'pull their plug', say "wait a minute, you are heading away from Jesus" and challenge their

---

[66] 1 Tim 2:5 New Living Translation, copyright © 1996, 2004, 2015 by Tyndale House Foundation
[67] Col 1:16 New Living Translation, copyright © 1996, 2004, 2015 by Tyndale House Foundation

teaching. If someone actually does, they may take an attitude that 'no one can tell me what's right.'

The issue is not the freedom to think outside the box, or to enjoy fresh revelation (we are all growing in our understanding of the Gospel), rather it is to miss the crucial fact that it is together we have the mind of Christ; this precious teaching is entrusted to a *body* of believers, in fact, the Body of Christ. The *ekklesia* should not wear straight jacket, rather a corporate priestly robe in which we share together the glory of God.

God has made provision for good teaching in his church. The words in Ephesians 4:11-12 make this clear:

> What God has in us, is gift wrapped to the world: some are commissioned to pioneer, others are gifted prophetically, some as announcers of good news, some as shepherds with a real gift to care and nurture, and others have a gift to ignite instruction through revelation knowledge. Each expression of his gift is to fully equip and enable you for the work of the ministry so that you may mutually contribute in your specific function to give definition to the visible body of Christ.[68]

There is something shared, held-in-common, mutual in this. There is a humility in 'accurately handling the word of truth' (2 Tim 2:15 NASB) in the rightly understood 'fear of the Lord.' This is not a cringing fear of a moody, vindictive God, who will slap us down if we deviate slightly in our sharing. Rather is an appreciation of the Glory that is pure goodness 'because he is a billion volts of beauty and gladness

---

[68] Ephesians 4:11-12 Mirror Bible (paraphrase by Francois du Toit)

and goodness and sweetness and happiness and love, and you are a little two-volt fuse.'[69] There is a holy wonder in this message handed down.

The issue is not the *ekklesia* per se, but how we have seen it. John Crowder said at a recent conference:

> If you've been hurt by the church, and experienced spiritual abuse – welcome to the club – we're still created for body life. He *does* give us good shepherds. He doesn't expect us to walk out this life alone. There is community for us, there is safe relationship for us.[70]

That God should entrust such a precious message to the likes of you and I may constantly amaze us. But he also allowed the scriptures to be written on parchments and scrolls that have only survived in pieces and scraps, to be compiled, assembled, translated, interpreted and then revised again and again as more accurate versions are discovered[71]. He must have been confident that – as he remains with us ('I will send you another like me' and 'it is better for you that I go away') – that Holy Spirit would guide us as a collective body and allow us to steward what was important through the ages. This allows for a maturing of revelation and understanding through the community, an un-packing of the treasures in the Good News.

---

[69] John Crowder at the Creed conference, Bristol 2019
[70] Telos week, Charlestown, Cornwall UK May 2022
[71] The Septuagint is 1000 years older than the Masoretic text (which formed the basis for the mainline translations such as the Authorised Version) and reflects a Hebrew textual form that predates the Masoretic by a millennium. There are also Aramaic scriptures that show another parallel textual tradition (which Brian Simmonds draws on in The Passion Translation)

There we discover another dimension of *ekklesia*; it is a continuum with those that have passed before and those who will follow. A friend remarked to me recently that the reason that ancient church buildings in Britain are often surrounded by graveyards is not meant to be a morbid reminder of the transitory nature of life, rather it is a recognition of the 'cloud of witnesses' that surround us. We together with them give testimony to the Life that flows though the Son of God, so that others on this planet who have not yet awakened to their redeemed identity might also encounter the healing and wholeness he has won! God believed it was safe to entrust that to us.

We have been experimenting with daily offices in our worship, amid what is often a vibrant and informal style (see Appendix). As part of that we have paraphrased the Creed in our own words:

> We believe in one God, the Father Almighty whose goodness is more than enough for all, filling the universe with gifts of love and resounding through our lives with praise.

> We believe in one Lord Jesus Christ, forever the only Son of God, sharing one essence with the Father, dazzling in pure light. He sang everything into being, which only exists through him.

> In order that we may be healed and made whole, he took on human flesh through the Spirit's power, born through Mary, a humble virgin.

> He fully drank the cup of our sin and rejection, yielding himself to death by our hands on a Roman cross. Three days later he rose to life again – as the scriptures had promised – and then

ascended to the Father's side, that we may be seated with him in heavenly places. He will return to set things right for all; his kingdom of love, joy and righteousness will last forever.

We believe in God's Holy Spirit of Truth, through whose Lordship everything is brought into fruition as the Father and Son desire, and is worshipped with the Godhead.

The Spirit spoke through God's prophets about these things. We recognise the church was brought into being by Christ, to faithfully pass on the apostolic message.

We understand that we have been baptised into Christ, fully forgiven, and are stirred by his Life in us; breathing, laughing, living fully in our world that all may know God's harvest of love.

Oh yes![72]

---

[72] A version of the Creed compiled by David Hewitt, inspired by one written by Andrew Metcalfe

FIVE | WELFARE

While we each have individual access to the Godhead and are respectively loved and valued in our unique contribution, when God deals with mankind, he usually does it to the corporate group. Hence most of the instructions and teachings are delivered to 'you' (plural) rather than 'you' (singular). Much is made of how we relate to one-another and of how *together* we display the glory of God. Paul refers to us as an interconnected body. Peter describes us like a new 'temple' made by living stones 'co-constructed, and seamlessly joined into a spiritual house'[73] within which we are one with the Lord. It seems therefore that the *ekklesia* has the opportunity to demonstrate something exceptional about welfare (love-in-action) both among believers and to the wider community, as the glory shines from this living temple.

When God makes provision of manna for the Children of Israel in the desert (Exodus 16), he makes clear that no one was to be left out; '…the one who gathered much did not have too much, and the one who gathered little did not have too little. Everyone had gathered just as much as they needed.' (NIV) There was a sense of provision for the community in this[74] – enough for everyone's need but not their greed.

When the early church gathered around the temple courts and had meals from home to home in Acts 2, we read 'All the believers were

---

[73] From 1 Pet 2:5 Mirror Bible (paraphrase by Francois du Toit)
[74] Walter Brueggemann made the point about the corporate, counter-cultural nature of the Bible in the Inverse Podcast 2019

together and had everything in common. They sold property and possessions to give to anyone who had need.'(NIV)

The *ekklesia* has this heritage; one of demonstrating the all-sufficient abundance of God through shared provision to the needy and vulnerable, care for the hurting and food for the hungry. Despite its many faults through the centuries (as mentioned in the opening section, and acknowledged by contemporary Christian writers[75]), the church has nonetheless been at the forefront of countless acts of mercy, from the open doors of the early monastics, the remote mission hospitals in developing lands to the many unsung, local groups that love and serve in communities across the globe. Food banks and homeless hostels are frequent expressions these days.

I would suggest that in a world that is showing itself increasingly vulnerable with fractured communities at so many levels, the encouragement of inter-related, inter-dependent groups who care for one another is what the Father, Son and Holy Spirit want. These may not necessarily have the label 'Christian', however as those who have awakened to Christ-in-us, he is in us as salt and light as we participate in every area of daily life.

The *ekklesia* is a prophetic demonstration of this welfare! The Greek word best describing this is *koinonia,* which Thayer's Lexicon defines as 'fellowship, association, community, communion, joint participation.' Of these definitions, the most accurate is 'community,' or better, 'a commune.' The adjective, *koine,* means 'common' and the verb, *koinoneo,* means 'to hold in common.'

---

[75] Brian McLaren highlights how 'The stories we typically tell ourselves about Christianity keep us living in our comfortable delusion of innocence' in his book Do I *stay* Christian? (Hodder & Stoughton 2022)

This communal approach may make some libertarians nervous, seeming closer to communism than capitalism, nevertheless there have been some bold examples of believers doing just that.

Clarence Jordan was one such exponent of radical community, and in the 1940s wrote:

> It is evident that this is by no means the philosophy of Russian communism. While communism is the result in both cases, the motivation is vastly different. One is the voluntary product of love, the other the involuntary product of force.

He went on to defend this approach:

> Such, then, was the meaning of Christian fellowship for the early disciples. Whether or not we can have it depends largely upon our willingness to pay the price.[76]

Koinonia Farm was founded in Georgia, USA in 1942 by Clarence & Florence Jordan and Martin & Mabel England as a 'demonstration plot for the Kingdom of God.' For them, this meant an intentional community of believers sharing their lives and resources, following the example of the first Christian communities as described in the Acts of the Apostles. Others linked to them, and with a commitment to equality and pacifism they welcomed people from all backgrounds and across the racial spectrum. This was at a considerable cost, as

---

[76] *Spring 1946 issue of* Prophetic Religion: A Journal of Christian Faith and Action. A farmer, preacher, and bible scholar, Clarence Jordan (1912-1969) founded Koinonia Farm, a pacifist interracial Christian community in Georgia, in 1942. See more at https://www.koinoniafarm.org/

they were opposed by the KKK and other politically minded groups. Their ministry evolved over the years, forming Habitat for Humanity International and other offshoots, to support the homeless and refugees. Eighty years later Koinonia Farm is still thriving, with among other things an active mail-order business. While not being presented necessarily as a blueprint, we recognise that their vision is simple and inspiring:

Love Through Service to Others • Joy Through Generous Hospitality • Peace Through Reconciliation

When we recognise that the living Jesus dwells within us and is the head of the Body, intent on producing the fruit of the kingdom throughout laid-down lives, then *ekklesia* can be an exciting place to connect!

In reading John 15 – in which Jesus declares himself the True Vine – we may have been concerned at the descriptions of pruning; the unfruitful branches are only good for being 'cast into the fire'. However, the emphasis of this wonderful passage is that we *are* dwelling, abiding, in the Vine; as usual by stark contrast Jesus is saying how useless any alternative would be; it would just be like firewood. Abiding is about resting in him, not seeking to make things happen though our own efforts but allowing the overflow of the abundant life he has placed within us form the beautiful fruit. After all, it is just natural for vine-branches to bear luscious, juicy grapes when growing from the stock of the True Vine.

The emphasis is *not* on the outward form; this can express itself in multifarious ways. Jesus also said the life of the Spirit within us would be like a 'gushing fountain' or 'geyser', so we should expect a vibrant array of expressions of *ekklesia.* Let's allow love to be the core of our gathered groups, seeing Christ in each person, valuing them and encouraging them in a non-judgemental way. That doesn't mean that we have to agree with everything they may think or do. Jesus loved each person he encountered and extended forgiveness – even while being tortured to death on a cross. His harsh words were for the religious group who rejected him because he did not meet their 'doctrine of beliefs', who would not receive the grace offered to them.

Our Christ-centred communities can offer that sense of practical, mutual support that is absent in so many urban settings. It does not have to look the same as the Koinonia Farm example; each setting is different. If the core values are there, then they can be evident whether we live on the same physical land or not. The intent to connect, encourage, love and walk in harmony with can exist whatever shape our group may take. What matters is that they are authentic, that when people touch our lives, they 'taste' the Father, Son and Holy Spirit in all we do and speak.

The three case studies that follow the next section show how a vibrant *ekklesia* can exist – aware of both our union with Jesus and one another, valuing each member – and display his glory through our gathered communities.

SIX | REFORMATION

Several excellent writers have suggested that what we are undergoing is in fact a new reformation. If *ekklesia* can survive in the 21st Century then this is simply vital, we must embrace radical change. Our worldview is constantly changing – developments in quantum physics, DNA research, social media and technology, not to mention climate crises, wars and financial instability – and a one-size-fits-all approach will not be relevant.

This new reformation has a sound Christology at its core; it begins with an encounter with the Lord of Lords. We don't start with the religions of the world, assessing their relative worth, and arrive at Jesus, we start with encountering him. We don't start with scripture and work towards Jesus, we start with Jesus and see all of scripture though the lens of Christ. We don't start with church structures and add in Jesus, we start with Jesus and see what emerges. We don't start with science or philosophy and work out what we think about Jesus, we start with Jesus and appreciate what we can learn through those disciplines. And when we speak of Jesus, the Father and the Holy Spirit are there too – this all began in the heart of the Trinity.

What about the negatives from our experience to date? Brian Maclaren says that if we walk away from Christianity because of the excesses, we find the same excesses exist in all other areas of human life.[77] He calls instead for 'anticipatory Christianity' that is not conservative and change resistant but leans into the future. I don't

---

[77] Brian McLaren Do I *stay* Christian? (Hodder & Stoughton 2022)

necessarily agree with all his views, but he makes a robust challenge to narrow, conservative evangelicalism or contemporary charismatic culture.

Jesus presented a radical truth to the disciples and crowds on the hillside near Galilee; unless you 'eat my flesh and drink my blood', you can have no part of me:

> Jesus replied to them, "Listen to this eternal truth: Unless you eat the body of the Son of Man and drink his blood, you will not have eternal life. Eternal life comes to the one who eats my body and drinks my blood, and I will raise him up in the last day. For my body is real food for your spirit and my blood is real drink. The one who eats my body and drinks my blood lives in me and I live in him. The Father of life sent me, and he is my life. In the same way, the one who feeds upon me, I will become his life. I am not like the bread your ancestors ate and later died. I am the living Bread that comes from heaven. Eat this Bread and you will live forever!"[78]

All we are should only be seen through the fact that we were co-crucified and co-raised with him, in order that the 'old Adam' be put to death, that we may now live in and through the Last Adam.

In the village of Iffley, now a suburb of Oxford in England, there is an amazing modern stained-glass window by Roger Wagner that depicts Christ on the cross, *superimposed* on the Tree of Life. At its base the River of Life flows out, surrounded by images of creation. This

---

[78] John 6:53-58 The Passion Translation®. Copyright © 2017, 2018, 2020 by Passion & Fire Ministries, Inc.

beautifully illustrates the message Jesus was giving us; the core to 'eating and drinking' is to live from the source of life. Jesus body and blood is the Tree of Life, offered for all.

Perhaps we have over-complicated what was so simple that even a child could understand it. Paul Golf notes that we should not 'over define' – after all, we are speaking of mystical truths here – but focus instead on our union with the Godhead and our participation in the Divine Life. He says, 'encounter is like defibrillation'; it shocks the heart to restore a normal heartbeat.

Earthly human life has always been fragile and transient. Yet it's the global effect of current trends and challenges that are raising the stakes in our time. The world-system does not have the answers and humanity is crying out for help. However, Paul states in Ephesians 3:10-11 that we have a unique contribution:

> His intent was that now, through the church, the manifold wisdom of God should be made known to the rulers and authorities in the heavenly realms, according to his eternal purpose that he accomplished in Christ Jesus our Lord. (NIV)

> Every invisible authority and government in the arena of the heavenlies were confronted with the display of God's genius. The ekklesia disperses the varied magnitude of God like a prism, in human form. This is mirrored in Jesus Christ our Master, who is the face-bread of the ages. He is the eloquent exhibit of God's prophetic thought. (MIR)

Active, interdependent, vibrant expressions of 'reconstructed *ekklesia*' that celebrate the finished work of Christ, are the communities the Godhead has always intended as vessels to share the Gospel of love. As we lean into the future, lets re-imagine what is meant to be the Body of Christ, recognising the presence of the Father, Son and Holy Spirit in all people as a starting point. In removing the artificial barriers that have made Jesus toxic to many, we can present the Saviour of the World and say 'awaken to the One who has loved you from the start.'

Maybe it's a period of 'rewilding' that is needed, to borrow a term from the conservationists. Letting go of harmful interventions and unnatural growth. Not forcing a result but rather allowing the Father, Son and Holy Spirit to nurture what grows naturally, i.e. by the inherent nature of their presence in us as image bearers. In the natural world this takes time and goes through various stages. As we go on, we can listen to their wisdom and prompting and respond positively to this growth, as they bring the gift of cultivation to the process. The Lord describes us in Isaiah as a 'well-watered garden' – gardening seems to be his delight (note how the Garden of Eden is the initial image he gives us of our intended environment, and it has been pointed out that after the resurrection he is again first identified as the 'gardener'). What grows there is by his life-source, not our own efforts. That's not to say we have no role, but rather to acknowledge that Christ has accomplished our salvation and now we participate in the joyful overflow!

I recognise that the route of deconstruction is necessary for many. We validate them and their journey and do not desire to shortcut the process. This document has not been so much about personal, faith deconstruction, rather about the case for the *ekklesia*. Yet deconstruction was never intended to be a destination; maybe it is part of the maturing process though which we come to know 'the truth of our being'. Brad Jersak has been on this journey himself and walked with many who have also been or are still on that path. In his excellent book 'Out of the Embers: Faith After the Great Deconstruction' he relates how this can be life changing:

> The highlights of the Exodus narrative—for Israel, for Jesus, for us— remind us that Christianity itself is an Exodus story, even when its hierarchs become the new Pharaoh, its structures the new pyramids, and its institutions the new Egypt...
>
> Whenever Christendom becomes a venue for spiritual slavery, the instinct for exodus shouldn't shock us. That just might be Moses calling, "Thus says the Lord God of Israel: 'Let My people go, that they may hold a feast to Me in the wilderness'" (Exodus 5:1 NKJV)...
>
> ...Many of my friends describe their deconstruction, even out of Christianity, as a second conversion—not unlike the mainline Protestants who experienced a 'second blessing' or the Catholic mystics who 'saw the light.' If what people are describing as their deconstruction sounds like just another word for conversion, that's because it often is...
>
> Our experiences of exodus, of awakening, of letting go, of transformation, of metamorphosis, and so forth, represent a familiar path—a spiritual tradition, believe it or not—that we

find at the very heart of the Christian story and echoed through the lives and testimonies of the saints.[79]

This new reformation is profoundly encouraging. Despite statistics and indications to the contrary, the Lord says to us

> ...But how could a loving mother forget her nursing child and not deeply love the one she bore? Even if a there is a mother who forgets her child, I could never, no never, forget you. Can't you see? I have carved your name on the palms of my hands!... Isaiah 49:15-16 (TPT)

If you find yourself isolated or alone in your faith, you may wish to see if there are a few others on the same path who you can meet up with, even if it is intermittently at first. Share the sacraments. If possible, move nearer and make the opportunities for gathering a more regular thing. Allow it to look like whatever it looks like, yet recognise Jesus at the core, in one another and in the community you live in.

I conclude with another statement from Baxter Kruger:

> What binds us together is the astonished heart. Astonished because we have met Jesus and his Father and the Holy Spirit in our own souls. We're drawn together because we want more: more shared life with Jesus, more clarity on who he is and who we are in him ... we begin to see church through his eyes.

---

[79] Brad Jersak 'Out of the Embers: Faith After the Great Deconstruction' (pg 51 – 52)

It is thus that we seek out one another. Jesus will build his *ekklesia*.

The next section includes examples of three new expressions of church that have developed over the last 10-15 years. There may be many similar churches I could have chosen from around the world, but these are current, grace-orientated communities that I know of. They are not presented as blueprints to follow and are not perfect, but they are examples of how non-hierarchical, relational, participatory Spirit-led *ekklesia* can still thrive in the 21st century.

SEVEN | BERN WEST COMMUNITY
Bern, Switzerland

Development of satellite church groups

Interview with Ivan Schmid

Bern West Community actually started with a clear model inherited from one of the Swiss pioneers of the house church movement. I was a strong believer in the 'right method'! It was already quite community-based, but its stated purpose was *to plant churches*. However, I would say we have since changed; that can never be the main reason why we are together! The reason we are together is because we love one another, we are the Body of Christ in one place; we are not purpose-driven, we are relationship driven.

Initially we had a team of 7 people who moved into the same neighbourhood. It had some high-rise buildings; it was not a plush area. I was quite driven though; the whole thing was 'how can we church-plant, how can we reach the people, how many people will get saved?' and after a few years I just go so tired.

However, there was another community at the Looslistrasse very nearby, led by a guy called Dominic Frei; they started about the same time. We initially tried to do various programmes together, but it didn't work – we had too many different ideas – but when the revelation of the Gospel began to sink in, that Christ has finished the work and we now live in the overflow, in union with him, a group of the younger guys from both churches began to meet regularly and just take communion together. I began to realize that if the Gospel is about relationships, then that is where we should start! Some of us began to gather before work and the two communities began to merge (between 2011-2014). It was the time that the revelation of the simpler Gospel began to really impact most – not all – but that made it possible; as we began to look away from the methods, the structures, whether it was a 'success' or not, and instead church became fun, there was a lot of joy and freedom. A common problem, it seems to me, is that many churches have their own methods, teaching, doctrine ... as long as you agree you are welcome, if not, you have to move on. This a totally different approach.

It took a while for people to really engage with this new revelation. We decided to spend a period of time – three to four years – just circling around the truth of the Gospel! There was a series of visiting speakers who majored on this. At that time, we were all living close. It's a bit more spread out now, and in fact one group is detaching from us (their focus is slightly different, but that's OK). Yet we still have this idea of living close by one another if we can.

We are three main satellite groups now, all within 5-10 kms distance – two in the city and one in a rural area adjacent. One group, Bümpliz, is in a block of 50 flats, in which 10 belong to people in the community. Then in the Bethlehem district there is a building with about 8 apartments and a café, with people also living around about, which is also next to a meeting space which we hire. The rural group is more dispersed, and there are still others who are spread out across the city and join into which ever group they prefer.

We have noticed that when satellites are smaller, people are much more connected and faithful in attending! When it gets over 100-120 some started dropping out – it's too loud, too many kids etc. – but with less, there is a greater sense of belonging. Our local groups are around 30-40 people (kids included). We have been meeting as a combined group once a month, and another time as separate groups.

Of course, there are challenges. Some look back at the time of transition as 'the Glory time', with a lot of 'drunkenness' in the Spirit, and now see themselves moving on from this foundation. And in my opinion, we became a bit intimidated for a while by those who were less comfortable with the freedom. But then we noticed the negative effects; it started to get dry again, it was becoming boring! So, we have intentionally returned to times of just 'drinking', circling around/talking about the Gospel – and I see many reawakening, it's so good!

We have a team of elders that lead – currently all couples – without one person having 'the last word'. Of course, there are some with a gift of leadership; we let people take turns to lead, and if someone carries the initiative, we recognize the anointing on them. Looking more widely, we find that there are more people who like to follow than take the initiative though! Families with young kids seem to find all their energy taken up. Yet some have extra energy. I observe that a generation that grew up with computer gaming and more sedentary childhoods, seem less willing; maybe they need to be shown how to form physical community?

I've noticed also that people who are less connected to community tend to wander away from the Gospel. The Trinitarian approach must be a starting point for our gatherings. It can even be online, if necessary, but an encouragement to regularly 'drink' is vital. We are born to share this message. Look out for the life and let the structure follow that. If we let things get too theoretical, it can lead to divisions; everyone has an opinion or a verse for this or that. Our background, personal preference, teaching history, views on 'controversial subjects' can all feed into this – when this happens, we are reminded to go back to the basics of the Gospel.

At one time we gathered in a circle and gave everyone chance to speak for 10 minutes with no interruptions. As to who started, we picked a number. Our aim was not to fix things, rather to properly hear one another, no pressure; we came to see what we all actually agreed upon. How do we come to consensus? It comes from loving one another. We want leaders who are truly servants – they don't need to be seen but serve the flow. There is a shift from 'I am scared of you, I need to control you, corral you, show you what to do' to 'you are a New Creation, you share in the mind of Christ.'

While we like to gather with all ages, we have something specifically for kids led by different people at each of our monthly gatherings. We also have a Friday evening time just for them, their language, their questions, games, stories. We practice community life just for them, eating together, contributions geared so that they understand the Gospel, inviting different parents to come and tell their life stories, practicing prophetic listening for each other etc. We also link to other city kids' groups, co-working with them, as we don't have the manpower to provide everything. If there are differences in emphasis, we encourage our kids just to live what we believe. Kids must be a focus, certainly.

We notice a gap in the 16-26 age group. Many young adults 26+ came to us through the Gloryfest events we organized and the Ministry School we ran; they came and stayed.

Looking further afield, we also support some missions in India and elsewhere. We take teams to visit these quite regularly.

EIGHT | HILLSIDE COVENANT COMMUNITY
Fort Wayne, USA

One joyful expression of a New Ecclesiology

by Matt Spinks

Hillside Covenant Community started in 2005 in response to some strong nudging of Holy Spirit and quite a disillusionment with what seemed to be the state of the majority of the church worldwide! A small group of friends, just a few years out of high school, began to email each other – after growing up in mainstream Christianity and afterward being exposed to more modern non-denominational charismatic expressions of the faith. Our initial goal was to 'forget all that we thought we knew, so we could re-learn what it meant to be true followers of Jesus Christ.' We felt like we had yet to see anything like how the church was living in the book of Acts, the miracles, the salvations, the awe, the shared life.

After emailing one another for a period of six months or so, we decided to all move to the same neighbourhood in Fort Wayne, Indiana USA to attempt to 're-learn what it means to be a Christian, and to re-learn church.' Initially, our expression became more and more intense, more and more religious. We began to meet seven nights a week, we encouraged strict discipline, and especially emphasized structured prayer and repentance as a means by which we were going to transform the world. Eventually, we ended up being profoundly impacted by Grace, and an understanding that Jesus Christ had already done something *so* significant to save the world. Our lives and church expression began to thrive and be filled with joy under this Grace revelation, with many of the 'book of Acts type expressions' finally happening in our midst.

We only started with about seven or eight folks … We've met in dozens of locations, backyards, apartments, homes, a fire station, a kids Sunday school classroom and currently a converted outbuilding behind our home. It's been amazing, a dream come true for me. I wouldn't do any of it much differently than we did.

From the beginning of our gathering together, we knew we wanted more than just a once or twice a week formal meeting. We had all grown up experiencing various forms of traditional church and wanted life together instead. We were radical. We were naive; but we were sincere. The Acts 2:42-27 picture was quite an inspiration to us. Our hearts were to see the church become something transformative to society. If I'm honest, we're still just scratching the surface of what it means to live this stuff out.

One thing we noticed from the beginning was that a level of commitment was going to be needed to progress in life and community impact together. It stood out to us how little commitment there was in the current mindsets of Western Christians. The fear of becoming manipulative or cultish also stood out as a reason for that hesitancy toward commitment; a valid concern that we understood to some degree. The book *The Vision and the Vow* by Pete Grieg came to our attention in those early days, and we were deeply touched by the *Moravian Order of the Mustard*

Seed that Pete wrote about. We felt called to make a series of commitments to one another in a similar way. Our commitments especially emphasized that our community was going to live the Gospel together long term, with an expectation that everyone would commit to one another like a spiritual family. Each member received a ring as a sign of their commitment! Just like any family, this has resulted in many challenges, failures, and tough discussions. But, so far, the joys seem to have far outweighed the challenges. We certainly have had to be intentional about many things to avoid the pitfalls on various sides of being a committed spiritual community. Despite still stumbling at times, the living Message of God's Grace in Christ has proved sufficient for us!

When we first started meeting together, we had more of an eldership and small leadership that led from the front, or in separate leadership meetings. Over the years, as the message of Christ-in-all permeated our awareness, we shifted into something different. In 2014 we gathered for a series of reformational meetings where we voted that anyone who had been attending for more than nine months would essentially become a leader, with equal say and equal vote on the direction of the group. We decided to gather around a table on a regular basis, with no agenda other than to be together in the Holy Spirit. We adopted a 'talking stick' and had 'voting sticks' to help guide our fellowship and decision making. If someone wants worship, they can begin to lead it. If someone wants to prophesy, they can do it. The format of our gatherings is currently a place where each person who has joined the group is able to express their heart, their views, their ideas, their inspiration for the whole group to hear, to consider, and to be ministered to by – we recognise that Christ dwells in each other!

All the expressions are welcome at the table, and we each participate and give room for one another. If someone wants to propose a project or change to the group, all those who have attended for more than nine months can vote on it. The community feels more like a tribe where every voice is heard and encouraged to participate. This is our model up to this day. We also just hang out at random times throughout the week, attempting to be more than 'church friends', but real friends. We do birthdays together, do street ministry, volunteer together, go on trips for mission and vacation, text, call, have BBQs, and do whatever friends do.

Our goals in doing church life have always been to experience life like they did in Acts 2:42-27, to have a place where the lonely could be put into family – actual family (Ps. 68:6) – and to see transformation in the society around us. This necessitated more than just a random 'church hopping', 'conference attending' mentality. We have attempted to wisely take the risks of looking like a cult (as well as genuinely *avoiding* cult-like tendencies within ourselves) and triggering folks fears of commitment. Again, for us the rewards have far outweighed the risks.

This has taken quite a bit more than what is expected from random churchgoers in some ways; in other ways it feels so much easier than the church I grew up with. It has been such a blessing having moved to live close to one another (most of us live within a couple of miles of one another).

Hillside has always been an 'intentional community', not just another 'church', not even just a 'group of friends'. Our heart was to purposefully be the kingdom of God, in each other's lives regularly with kingdom intention, a focused greenhouse for Glory! Intentional community can be beautifully spontaneous and organic and free flowing. But to see it stay around long term, it just *has* to be intentional, meaning it does take purposeful prioritizing and contemplative planning. I believe this vision is just true normal 'church' life, or the normal body life of Christ in a neighbourhood setting. It is not something better than, or really that different from what I believe God planned to exist all over the world, in smaller community settings everywhere. I just see Hillside as one immediate family, amid a global extended family of Jesus all over the world! In fact, all humanity is our family! But there is a way to live out healthy body life amid an immediate spiritual family of real people, with real names, and real addresses, people you plan to see almost every day! Once the immediate family is established, then from there we find our place in the global extended family.

It has also taken quite a bit of intentional teaching and impartation by the Holy Spirit to keep us joyful, communicating, and in love! The Trinitarian Gospel of Grace has made all the difference in keeping us spiritually satisfied in God, and full of real-life grace for one another during it all. The incarnational unconditional love approach to community that we see in Christ has empowered us to enjoy everyday life, and welcome everyone to the table day after day, week after week. To be honest, we're having so much fun, my heart burns to see everyone on earth come into this kind of community life!

I believe that we, as Hillside, are even being a manifestation of God in the earth right now, to set forth a beautiful example of what normal body life can be like. A place where we are not controlling, we are giving everyone an equal voice, we are staying organic and natural, *and yet* still calling people to gather regularly and planning our lives intentionally around each other in specific ways. We are not spiritual anarchists, in which there is no structure or organization (though that is not necessarily wrong). We are rather a 'freedom-based intentional community!'

NINE | WELLSPRINGS COMMUNITY
Edinburgh, Scotland

A blank sheet for a fresh start

by David Hewitt

Contrary to the other examples, we started with a building. In May 2006 David & Maggie had never thought about moving home, but by the end of June they had sold their house and purchased a former Victorian church on the edge of Edinburgh. It had been used as a piano workshop and warehouse for 15 years, had a resident population of rats and needed much renovation.

Their daughter Rachel had been having a 'day out with Jesus' on the beach in nearby East Lothian. She was coming back on the bus and saw a For Sale notice on the building. As an avid 24/7 intercessor with a heart to start a 'boiler room', she was intrigued. She was chatting to her mentor soon after, who was encouraging and 'gave her permission to dream'. A day later she went to see it with some friends. As they wandered around the building, which was crammed with pianos and other musical instruments, they sensed 'this place needs to be released for worship again'!

She phoned up the agent and was emailed the particulars. She asked her parents whether they wanted to come and see it too, so one sunny afternoon at the beginning of June they went out and had a look (thinking 'this is a fun, zany idea, but would be impossible'). However, as they wandered around it, they felt something of excitement stir within. Maggie and David had carried a heart for creativity in prayer and worship for several years, and sensed God had spoken to them in scriptures, dreams and prophecies. As they walked praying around the area afterwards, conversing with the Lord, a 'seed was planted' for a House of Prayer. As well as a venue for prayer & worship, they could see it being a place for Movement in Worship [dance] workshops. It was also in a location designated to be a major growth area to the east of Edinburgh, and an ideal location for something new.

With David's architectural input and a supportive team of builders, we moved into a loft-style apartment created in the roof of the building in March 2007. Over the next year the voluminous space was upgraded and subdivided to create also a large Upper Room, a two-bedroom Garden Flat, four extra ground floor bedrooms, a schoolroom (for an educational charity we knew) and a Prayer Room. These first few years were marked by many exciting examples of God's provision (for example, the first year of heating ended up being provided free by the energy provider, a company came and resurfaced the car park as a gift and we were given some free carpeting plus a 100 chairs).

We had always had a heart for local church. Initially 13 people moved with us to live nearby, many just two minutes away or living within the building (now named 'Wellsprings'), and we had a sense of having been given a blank sheet; Wellsprings Community was born. Yet over the first decade, we found ourselves going though quite a transition, embracing an understanding of the gospel that was unmistakably

Trinitarian and grace-empowered through the Finished Work of Jesus. We grew in numbers; most grasped this quickly, others took time (and are still on that journey), a few moved on. We were privileged to have a steady stream of excellent speakers and teachers pass through and became a venue for some significant conferences that broadened this understanding. Along with this we've hosted many worship weekends and, with other friends, held some summer events called Glory in the Cowshed (in a barn in rural Perthshire).

The Community still has a creative flavour, with a heart for prayer and worship; however, rather than this being something *driven* it has now become a joyful overflow of who we are in Christ, drinking from the fountain within. When we gather it tends to be 'in the round', to facilitate participation and with a free flowing, rolling worship (with space for art, dance, percussion, sounds….). The 'shape' of the church has changed over the years, as has the pattern of gathering; some weeks we meet outdoors and go for a walk together plus we often have meals together. For several years we had a monthly Sunday gathering in a large local café offering live music and connecting with whoever was around (we termed the evening Spirit Rhythms).

Sharing communion has become a regular way of emphasising our participation in the Divine nature, and during the Covid lockdown we developed several contemporary liturgies based loosely on Celtic offices and practices. While a contemplative side has definitely emerged, we have never let go of our charismatic heritage; there's much 'drinking' and joy!

David has avoided the title 'pastor', seeing this as a function rather than a title, and continues to work part-time as an architect. He and Maggie gather with a steering group occasionally to agree on key decisions, but have always promoted a non-hierarchical style of leadership, seeing it more as an inverted pyramid, undergirding and releasing.

One of the challenges we have experienced is the gradual dispersal of homes through job moves and house sales etc. Most people still live within ten minutes travel, though a few do have to cross the city to come. We have found the need to be more *intentional* about gathering and have developed some new ways of connecting during the week, in homes and in the Prayer Room. Some Polish members moved back to Poland plus a few other key people passed away and were 'promoted to the cloud of witnesses'– our size reduced by about a quarter. We are still quite small in size, yet I would say closer than ever in sense of family and participation. People look out for one another, give when there are needs, pray consistently when others are under pressure. Pastoring and mentoring take place without the need for positions or titles.

Back in 2006 I felt the Lord drop into my heart the term 'Communities of the Spirit'. I think that is something the Godhead wanted to bring about in Wellsprings; a sense of Spirit-led gathering, knowing there is now no separation, we are *already* in the Holy Place. The emphasis on our union as one with Christ has transformed the orientation of the Community; seeing Christ in all has enabled us to embrace our connection with others without a sense of 'them and us'. We may not be large, but God has consistently spoken of us being an influence in the nation. As anyone who has shared a room with a mosquito knows, size is not everything!

The following appendices contain simple liturgies or offices that we adapted or developed over the past few years.

i. MORNING OFFICE

Choose someone to read the sections in italics. All join in the sentences in bold.

+ In the name of the Father, and of the Son, and of the Holy Spirit.
Amen

LEADER
Opening Sentences

Colossians 1:11-13 (MIRROR)
You are empowered in the dynamic of God's strength;
his mind is made up about you!
He enables you to be strong in endurance and
steadfastness with joy.
We are grateful to the Father who qualified us to participate
in the complete portion of the inheritance of the saints in the light.
He rescued us from the dominion of darkness and relocated us into
the kingdom where the love of his Son rules.

ALL The Lord's Prayer (adapted from the Passion*)
Abba Father, dwelling in the heavenly realms,
May the glory of your name
Be the centre on which our lives turn.
Manifest your kingdom reign and cause your every purpose to
Be fulfilled on earth, just as it is fulfilled in heaven.
And give us the continual bread of abundance.
Forgive our sins, as we ourselves release forgiveness

to those who have wronged us.
Rescue us from every ordeal
And set us free from evil.
For you are the King who rules
with power and glory forever.
Amen.

ALL Declaration of faith

We believe and trust in God the Father Almighty.
We believe and trust in Jesus Christ His Son.
We believe and trust in the Holy Spirit.
We believe and trust in the Three in One.

LEADER

You are the peace of all things calm,
You are the place to hide from harm.
You are the light that shines in dark,
You are the heart's eternal spark.
You are the door that's open wide,
You are the guest who waits inside.
You are the light, the truth, the way,
You are our Saviour this very day.

MEDITATION (read by a member of the Community)

COMMUNION (find some bread & wine)

LEADER

"I have handed down to you what came to me by direct revelation from the Lord himself. The same night in which he was handed over, he took bread and gave thanks. Then he distributed it to the disciples and said, "Take it and eat your fill. It is my body, which is given for you. Do this to remember me." He did the same with the cup of wine after supper and said, "This cup seals the new covenant with my blood. Drink it—and whenever you drink this, do it to remember me." Whenever you eat this bread and drink this cup, you are retelling the story, proclaiming our Lord's death until he comes."
(1 Corinthians 11:23-26 TPT)

ALL

Thank you, Lord, for becoming man and laying down your life for us, giving your body for us, redeeming our original value, identity, and innocence; dying our death and defining the life we now live.

LEADER (Share the bread)

Take this bread to declare you are included in Christ.

ALL

Thank you, Lord, for shedding your blood for us.
We are declaring our joint inclusion in your death and resurrection, confirming our redeemed innocence.

LEADER (Share the wine)
Take this wine to declare your redeemed innocence in Christ.

May the peace of the Lord Christ go with you,
wherever He may send you.
May He guide you through the difficult places,
protect you through the storms of life.
May He bring you home delighting
at the wonders He has shown you.
May He bring you home laughing
once again into our doors.

+ In the name of the Father, and of the Son, and of the Holy Spirit.
Amen

Wellsprings version, adapted from various Celtic offices, using the Mirror Word and the Passion Translation. *The Lord's prayer is a version amalgamated from renderings in both Matthew and Luke, with an interpretation of 'daily bread' by Colin Symes.

ii. EVENING OFFICE

Choose someone to read the sections in italics. All join in the sentences in bold.

**+ In the name of the Father, and of the Son, and of the Holy Spirit.
Amen**

LEADER
The Sacred Three
To save
To shield
To surround
The hearth
The home
This night
And every night.

ALL
**God, I invite your searching gaze into my heart. Examine me
through and through; find out everything that may be hidden
within me. Put me to the test and sift through all my anxious cares.
See if there is any path of pain I'm walking on, and lead me back to
your glorious, everlasting way— the path that brings me back to
you.**
(Psalm 139:23-24 TPT)

LEADER
O Father, Son and Holy Spirit.

Thank you for forgiving us our sins.
O only Son of the heavenly Father,
Thank you for forgiving us our sins.
O God who is one,
O God who is true,
O God who is first,
O God who is one substance,
O God only mighty,
In three Persons, truly merciful,
Thank you for forgiving us our sins.

ALL

The Lord is my revelation-light to guide me along the way;
he's the source of my salvation to defend me every day.
I fear no one!
I'll never turn back and run, for you, Lord,
surround and protect me.
… I know that you are there for me, so I will not be shaken.
Here's one thing I crave from God,
the one thing I seek above all else:
I want the privilege of living with him every moment in his
house, finding the sweet loveliness of his face,
filled with awe, delighting in his glory and grace.
I want to live my life so close to him that he takes
pleasure in my every prayer.
In his shelter in the day of trouble, that's where you will find me,
for he hides me there in his holiness.
He has smuggled me into his secret place,
where I'm kept safe and secure – out of reach from all my enemies.

(extract from Psalm 27:1-5 TPT)

I peace will I lie down, entwined with you,
For it is you, O Lord,
You alone who makes me to rest secure.

Resting in union with you,
O God of grace, in peace we shall awake.

The peace of the Spirit
Be ours this night.
The peace of the Son
Be ours this night.
The peace of the Father
Be ours this night.
The peace of all peace
Be ours this night.

+ In the name of the Father, and of the Son, and of the Holy Spirit.
Amen

Adapted with permission from the Evening Office of the Northumbria Community, using the Passion Translation of the scriptures (Second Edition).

iii. MONDAY

Choose someone to read the sections in italics. All join in the sentences in bold.

+ In the name of the Father, and of the Son, and of the Holy Spirit. Amen

Opening Sentences LEADER
For there is one God and one Mediator who can reconcile God and humanity—the man Christ Jesus. He gave his life to purchase freedom for everyone. This is the message God gave to the world at just the right time. (1 Tim 2:5-6 NLT)

ALL The Lord's Prayer (adapted from the Passion*)
Abba Father, dwelling in the heavenly realms,
May the glory of your name
Be the centre on which our lives turn.
Manifest your kingdom reign and cause your every purpose to be fulfilled on earth, just as it is fulfilled in heaven.
And give us the continual bread of abundance.
Forgive our sins, as we ourselves release forgiveness to those who have wronged us.
Rescue us from every ordeal
And set us free from evil.
For you are the King who rules with power and glory forever.
Amen.

Declaration of faith
We believe and trust in God the Father Almighty.
We believe and trust in Jesus Christ His Son.
We believe and trust in the Holy Spirit.
We believe and trust in the Three in One.

LEADER (Celtic blessing from the first millennium)
You are the peace of all things calm,
You are the place to hide from harm.
You are the light that shines in dark,
You are the heart's eternal spark.
You are the door that's open wide,
You are the guest who waits inside.
You are the light, the truth, the way,
You are our Saviour this very day.

——

MEDITATION (a member of the Community shares something)

COMMUNION (find some bread & wine)

LEADER
We bless you, Lord God Almighty, Father, Son and Holy Spirit,
Creator of all, that through your goodness we have this bread and
wine to partake in, which earth has given and hands have made:
they will be to us our spiritual food and drink!

ALL
Thank you, Lord, for becoming man and laying down your life for
us, giving your body for us, redeeming our original value, identity,
and innocence; dying our death and defining the life we now live.

LEADER (Share the bread
Take this bread to declare you are included in Christ.

ALL
Thank you, Lord, for shedding your blood for us. We are declaring our joint inclusion in your death and resurrection, confirming our redeemed innocence.

LEADER (Share the wine)
Take this wine to declare your redeemed innocence in Christ.

LEADER (Blessing)
May the peace of the Lord Christ go with you,
wherever He may send you.
May He guide you through the difficult places,
protect you through the storms of life.
May He bring you home delighting
at the wonders He has shown you.
May He bring you home laughing
once again into our doors.

+ In the name of the Father, and of the Son, and of the Holy Spirit.
Amen

Wellsprings version, adapted from various Celtic offices, using the New Living Translation (NLT) *The Lord's prayer is a version amalgamated from renderings in Matthew and Luke, with an interpretation of 'daily bread' by Colin Symes.

iv. TUESDAY

Choose someone to read the sections in italics. All join in the sentences in bold.

**+ In the name of the Father, and of the Son, and of the Holy Spirit.
Amen**

Opening Sentences LEADER
My only boast is in the crucifixion of the Lord Jesus, our Messiah. In him I have been crucified to this natural realm; and the natural realm is dead to me and no longer dominates my life. (Gal 6:14 TPT)

ALL The Lord's Prayer (adapted from the Aramaic)

Beloved Father, who fills all realms

May you be honoured in me.

Let your divine rule come now

**Let your will come true in all the universe,
in the heavens, and on earth.**

**Give us all that we need for each day, and
Untangle the knots of unforgiveness that bind us within,**

As we also let go of the guilt of others

Let us not be lost in superficial things,

But let us be free from that what keeps us from our true purpose.

From you comes all rule, the strength to act,

and the song that beautifies all,
From age to age.
Amen.

ALL Declaration of faith
We believe and trust in God the Father Almighty.
We believe and trust in Jesus Christ His Son.
We believe and trust in the Holy Spirit.
We believe and trust in the Three in One.

LEADER (Celtic Blessing)
May the celebration of resurrected life bring new hope to your being. May the victory over earthly death turn your eyes to the promises of heaven. May the empty tomb help you to leave your sorrows at the foot of the cross. So that God's hope, promises and forgiveness reign in your life forever.

———

MEDITATION (a member of the Community shares something)

COMMUNION (find some bread & wine)

LEADER
Let me remind you then what we are actually celebrating in our fellowship meal: The night in which the Lord Jesus was betrayed, he took bread and gave thanks; breaking the bread into portions, he said, "Realize your association with my death, every time you eat, remember my body that was broken for you!" (1 Cor 11:23-24)

ALL

Thank you, Lord, for becoming man and laying down your life for us, giving your body for us, redeeming our original value, identity, and innocence; dying our death and defining the life we now live.

LEADER (Share the bread
Take this bread to declare you are included in Christ

ALL

Thank you, Lord, for shedding your blood for us. We are declaring our joint inclusion in your death and resurrection, confirming our redeemed innocence.

LEADER (Share the wine)
Take this wine to declare your redeemed innocence in Christ

LEADER (Blessing)
Deep peace of the running wave to you.
Deep peace of the flowing air to you.
Deep peace of the quiet earth to you.
Deep peace of the shining stars to you.
Deep peace of the gentle night to you.
Moon and stars pour their healing light on you.
Deep peace of Christ,
of Christ the light of the world to you.
Deep peace of Christ to you.

+ In the name of the Father, and of the Son, and of the Holy Spirit.
Amen

v. WEDNESDAY

Choose someone to read the sections in italics. All join in the sentences in bold.

+ In the name of the Father, and of the Son, and of the Holy Spirit.
Amen

Opening Sentences LEADER
The conclusion is clear: our righteousness has absolutely nothing to do with our ability to keep moral laws; it is the immediate result of what Jesus accomplished on mankind's behalf. This gives context to faith and finds expression in unhindered, face to face friendship with God! Jesus Christ is the head of this union! (Rom 5:1 Mirror)

ALL The Lord's Prayer (adapted from the Passion*)
Abba Father, dwelling in the heavenly realms,
May the glory of your name
Be the centre on which our lives turn.
Manifest your kingdom reign and cause your every purpose to be fulfilled on earth, just as it is fulfilled in heaven.
And give us the continual bread of abundance.
Forgive our sins, as we ourselves release forgiveness
to those who have wronged us.
Rescue us from every ordeal
And set us free from evil.
For you are the King who rules with power
and glory forever.
Amen.

ALL Declaration of faith

We believe and trust in God the Father Almighty.

We believe and trust in Jesus Christ His Son.

We believe and trust in the Holy Spirit.

We believe and trust in the Three in One.

LEADER (Celtic Easter Blessing)

The everlasting three-fold friendship of God,

Light of lights, has come and awakened our hearts

That we might live in the power of His grace.

———

MEDITATION (a member of the Community shares something)

———

COMMUNION (find some bread & wine)

LEADER

Let me remind you then what we are actually celebrating in our fellowship meal: The night in which the Lord Jesus was betrayed, he took bread and gave thanks; breaking the bread into portions, he said, "Realize your association with my death, every time you eat, remember my body that was broken for you!" (1 Cor 11:23-24)

ALL

Thank you, Lord, for becoming man and laying down your life for us, giving your body for us, redeeming our original value, identity, and innocence; dying our death and defining the life we now live.

LEADER (Share the bread)

Take this bread to declare you are included in Christ

ALL

Thank you, Lord, for shedding your blood for us. We are declaring our joint inclusion in your death and resurrection, confirming our redeemed innocence.

LEADER (Share the wine)

Take this wine to declare your redeemed innocence in Christ

LEADER (Blessing)

Continue today clothed in the strength of Christ,
Free to weave Christ's heavenly patterns on the earth
Free from fear of being overwhelmed,
Free to love and be loved

+ In the name of the Father, and of the Son, and of the Holy Spirit.

Amen

Wellsprings version, adapted from various Celtic offices, using the Mirror Word paraphrase and the Passion Translation. *The Lord's prayer is a version amalgamated from renderings in Matthew and Luke, with an interpretation of 'daily bread' by Colin Symes.

vi. THURSDAY

**+ In the name of the Father, and of the Son, and of the Holy Spirit.
Amen**

Opening Sentences LEADER

See yourselves co-raised with Christ! Now ponder with persuasion the consequences of your co-inclusion in him. Relocate yourselves mentally! Engage your thoughts with Throne room realities where you are co-seated with Christ in the executive authority of God's right hand. Becoming affectionately acquainted with Throne room thoughts will keep you from being distracted again by the earthly realm. (Col 3:1-2 Mirror)

ALL The Lord's Prayer (adapted from the Aramaic)

Beloved Father, who fills all realms

May you be honoured in me.

Let your divine rule come now

**Let your will come true in all the universe,
in the heavens, and on earth.**

**Give us all that we need for each day, and
Untangle the knots of unforgiveness that bind us within,**

As we also let go of the guilt of others

Let us not be lost in superficial things,

But let us be free from that what keeps us from our true purpose.

From you comes all rule, the strength to act,
and the song that beautifies all,
From age to age.
Amen.

ALL Declaration of faith
We believe and trust in God the Father Almighty.
We believe and trust in Jesus Christ His Son.
We believe and trust in the Holy Spirit.
We believe and trust in the Three in One.

LEADER
Your union with Christ's death broke the control of the soul-ruled realm. You are now located in a fortress where your life is hidden with Christ in God! Today, may your mind be aligned with God's perspective on who you are, regardless of any circumstances that surround you.

MEDITATION (a member of the Community shares something)

COMMUNION (find some bread & wine)

LEADER
Let me remind you then what we are actually celebrating in our fellowship meal: The night in which the Lord Jesus was betrayed, he took bread and gave thanks; breaking the bread into portions, he said, "Realize your association with my death, every time you eat, remember my body that was broken for you!" (1 Cor 11:23-24)

Thank you, Lord, for becoming man and laying down your life for us, giving your body for us, redeeming our original value, identity, and innocence; dying our death and defining the life we now live.

LEADER (Share the bread)
Take this bread to declare you are included in Christ

ALL

Thank you, Lord, for shedding your blood for us. We are declaring our joint inclusion in your death and resurrection, confirming our redeemed innocence.

LEADER (Share the wine)
Take this wine to declare your redeemed innocence in Christ

LEADER (Blessing)
The peace of the Spirit
be ours this day.
The peace of the Son
be ours this day.
The peace of the Father
be ours this day.
The peace of all peace
be ours this day

+ In the name of the Father, and of the Son, and of the Holy Spirit.
Amen

vii. FRIDAY

Choose someone to read the sections in italics. All join in the sentences in bold.

+ In the name of the Father, and of the Son, and of the Holy Spirit.
Amen

Opening Sentences LEADER
My old identity has been co-crucified with Messiah and no longer lives; for the nails of his cross crucified me with him. And now the essence of this new life is no longer mine, for the Anointed One lives his life through me —we live in union as one! My new life is empowered by the faith of the Son of God who loves me so much that he gave himself for me, and dispenses his life into mine! (Gal 2:20 TPT)

ALL The Lord's Prayer (adapted from the Passion*)
Abba Father, dwelling in the heavenly realms,
May the glory of your name
Be the centre on which our lives turn.
Manifest your kingdom reign and cause your every purpose to be
fulfilled on earth, just as it is fulfilled in heaven.
And give us the continual bread of abundance.
Forgive our sins, as we ourselves release forgiveness
to those who have wronged us.
Rescue us from every ordeal and set us free from evil.
For you are the King who rules with power
and glory forever. Amen.

We believe and trust in God the Father Almighty.
We believe and trust in Jesus Christ His Son.
We believe and trust in the Holy Spirit.
We believe and trust in the Three in One.

LEADER

On this day, we live in the revelation that Jesus brought when he said 'On that day you will realise that I am in my Father, and you are in me, and I am in you.' Today sin-consciousness gives way to Son-consciousness!
Walk in the bliss of this truth.

―――

MEDITATION (a member of the Community shares something)

COMMUNION (find some bread & wine)

LEADER

Let me remind you then what we are actually celebrating in our fellowship meal: The night in which the Lord Jesus was betrayed, he took bread and gave thanks; breaking the bread into portions, he said, 'Realize your association with my death, every time you eat, remember my body that was broken for you!' (1 Cor 11:23-24)

ALL

Thank you, Lord, for becoming man and laying down your life for us, giving your body for us, redeeming our original value, identity, and innocence; dying our death and defining the life we now live.

LEADER (Share the bread)

Take this bread to declare you are included in Christ

ALL

Thank you, Lord, for shedding your blood for us. We are declaring our joint inclusion in your death and resurrection, confirming our redeemed innocence.

LEADER (Share the wine)

Take this wine to declare your redeemed innocence in Christ

LEADER (Blessing)

May the celebration of resurrected life bring hope to your being. May the victory over earthly death turn your eyes to the promises of heaven. May the empty tomb help you to leave your sorrows at the foot of the cross. So that God's hope, promises and forgiveness reign in your life forever.

+ In the name of the Father, and of the Son, and of the Holy Spirit.

Amen

Wellsprings version, adapted from various Celtic offices, using the Mirror Word paraphrase and the Passion Translation. *The Lord's prayer is a version amalgamated from renderings in Matthew and Luke, with an interpretation of 'daily bread' by Colin Symes.

viii. COMMUNION WITH THE WILD TRINITY

Choose someone to read the sections in italics. All join in the sentences in bold.

Introduction

The Celtic Christians often used the image of the wild goose to symbolize the work of the Holy Spirit, capturing that sense of wildness and freedom, that tendency of the Spirit to disrupt and surprise! It was that 'Wild Goose' charisma of the Holy Spirit that called Patrick back to Ireland, brought Columba to Iona, Aiden to Lindisfarne and Hilda to Whitby. Men and women of great faith and courage were empowered to make a huge impact upon the Britain of their day.

We cannot tame God, to fit into our plans and presumptions: rather we can respond to the wildness of the Godhead in their passion for mankind and creation.

*CS Lewis captured this sense in **The Lion, the Witch, and the Wardrobe:***

"They say Aslan is on the move..."

"He'll be coming and going" he had said. "One day you'll see him and another you won't. He doesn't like being tied down--and of course he has other countries to attend to. It's quite all right. He'll often drop in. Only you mustn't press him. He's wild, you know. Not like a tame lion."

Let's begin our communion by considering the wildness of the God of Creation, who we read in Genesis 1 brooded over the chaos of the deep. Psalm 104 captures the majesty of the God of Creation!

<u>ALL</u>
Extracts from Psalm 104 (TPT)
Each section read by a different person

1 Everything I am will praise and bless the Lord!

O Lord, my God, your greatness takes my breath away,

overwhelming me by your majesty, beauty, and splendour!

2 You wrap yourself with a shimmering, glistening light.

You wear sunshine like a garment of glory.

You stretch out the starry skies like a tapestry.

----

3 You build your balconies with light beams

and ride as King in a chariot you made from clouds.

You fly upon the wings of the wind.

4 You make your messengers into winds of the Spirit,

and all your ministers become flames of fire.

5 You, our Creator, formed the earth,

and you hold it all together so it will never fall apart.

———————————

24 O Lord, what an amazing variety of all you have created!

Wild and wonderful is this world you have made,

while wisdom was there at your side.

This world is full of so many creatures, yet each belongs to you!

25 And then there is the sea! So vast! So wide and deep—

swarming with countless forms of sea life, both small and great.

———————————

30 When you release your Spirit-Wind, life is created,

ready to replenish life upon the earth.

31 May God's glorious splendour endure forever!

May the Lord take joy and pleasure in all that he has made.

32 For the earth's overseer has the power to make it tremble;

just a touch of his finger and volcanoes erupt

as the earth shakes and melts.

33 I will sing my song to the Lord as long as I live!

Every day I will sing my praises to God.

34 May you be pleased with every sweet thought I have about you,

for you are the source of my joy and gladness.

Creator God, you brought forth the wonders of the universe to display your glory. From the very start, you intended to share this creation with us, men and women, who you created in your image. 'Even before the world was made, God loved us and chose us in Christ to be holy and without fault in his eyes.' Though we turned away from you, we are so grateful this day that 'while we were yet sinners, Christ died for us' to restore us to full relationship and heal the sense of separation in our hearts!

LEADER
John 14:20 (NIV)
On that day you will realize that I am in my Father,
and you are in me, and I am in you.

ALL
Galatians 2:20 (Passion Translation)
My old identity has been co-crucified with Christ and no longer lives. And now the essence of this new life is no longer mine, for the Anointed One lives his life through me—*we live in union as one*! My new life is empowered by the faith of the Son of God who loves me so much that he gave himself for me, *dispensing his life into mine*

—

Thank you, Jesus, for laying yourself down for me that I might fully partake in your great love and life without fear of separation or abandonment.

So I can give myself fully to you this day participating in the wildness of your love, knowing that by your faithful act I am included forever in you and invited into the 'Divine dance' of the Trinity

———

COMMUNION (find some bread & wine)
LEADER
The Lord is with us.

ALL
And His Spirit is here.

LEADER
Luke 22 (NIV) v19 And he took bread, gave thanks and broke it, and gave it to them, saying, 'This is my body given for you; do this to remember me.'

ALL
Thank you, Lord, for becoming man and laying down your life for us, giving your body for us, redeeming our original value, identity, and innocence; dying our death and defining the life we now live.

LEADER (Share the bread)
Take this bread to declare your inclusion in Christ.

v20 In the same way, after the supper he took the cup, saying,

'This cup is the new covenant in my blood, which is poured out for you.'

ALL

Thank you, Lord, for shedding your blood for us. We are declaring our joint inclusion in your death and resurrection, confirming our redeemed innocence.

LEADER (Share the wine)
Take this wine to declare your redeemed innocence in Christ

Let's all pray this Lord's Prayer paraphrased from the Aramaic (pausing after each line)

Beloved Father, who fills all realms

May you be honoured in me.

Let your divine rule come now

**Let your will come true in all the universe,
in the heavens, and on earth.**

**Give us all that we need for each day, and
Untangle the knots of unforgiveness that bind us within,**

As we also let go of the guilt of others

Let us not be lost in superficial things,

But let us be free from that what keeps us from our true purpose.

**From you comes all rule, the strength to act,
and the song that beautifies all,
From age to age.
Amen.**

Scripture taken from The Passion Translation (paraphrase) and the NIV, and the Lord's Prayer is a version of the Aramaic prayer of Jesus from *Prayers of the Cosmos* and *Revelations of the Aramaic Jesus* by Neil Douglas-Klotz copyright 1990, 2022. Reprinted with permission. All rights reserved. Website: https://abwoon.org

The Trinity is an icon created by Russian painter Andrei Rublev in the 15th century. It is his most well-known work and the most famous of all Russian icons, and it is regarded as one of the highest achievements of Russian art.

STUDY GUIDE

We are in an ongoing conversation: you may not agree with everything! Reconstructing Ecclesia is intended to provoke us further as we reconsider and reimagine the church. This guide prompts some questions for group discussion or further personal study, based on the chapters in the book. A reading list follows at the end.

1. Towards a new ecclesiology (p7)

What is the essential nature of the church, according to Baxter Kruger?
– what reasons would lead us to this definition?
– how does this affect the relationship of humanity with God?

In which key verse in John's Gospel does Jesus declare our union with him through of the work of the cross?

Why do we need churches anymore? (p9)

Define 'deconstruction'.
– why do you think this has affected the church so much in this era?
– what things have been brought into question?
– which of these things have affected you?

What does 'church' really mean? (p11)

In what ways was the Greek word *ekklesia* in common usage for Jesus and the apostles?
– what does the word suggest when we look at its root?
– how do we see Jesus and Paul applying this term, in teaching and practice?

A brief historical overview. (p15)

It is helpful to consider what influences have shaped the *ekklesia* through the centuries.
– describe the highs and lows of the church in the first three centuries.
– what brought about a change in direction, and how did that affect the way the early church functioned?
– what alternative strands could be found?
– how did the church split in 1054 AD?
– define the nature of 'Christendom'? What were the negative results?
– who shook the church up in 1517 AD? Name some of the outcomes.

Discuss the last 500 years since the Reformation. What are the joys and sorrows?
How can we view this with a compassionate and humble heart?

What then is the heart of *ekklesia*? (p20).

Read aloud the first paragraph of this section. Do you agree with this view?
– why can we struggle when discussing church today?

A list of values is proposed. Discuss how central you feel these are to the contemporary church.

Family (p21)

– where do we see the origins of this?
– what is the key nature of this Being?

George Macdonald spoke of how 'the Way of our being needs to align with the Truth of our being'. What do you think he meant by that? What aspect of Western culture is confronted head-on by this?
– how does the New Testament describe what this change looks like?

Discuss the statement that the *ekklesia* 'is in no way meant to be in hermetically sealed containers, but porous outward-looking communities...' (p24)
– what would lead us to state 'there is now no separation'?
– share some scriptures that underline this.
– where is the Godhead at work today?

We live in the internet age.
– how can this benefit *ekklesia*?
– identify some shortcomings.
– what aspects of *ekklesia* require physical connection?

What other things are key? (p27)

Why might **food** be an important ingredient of *ekklesia*?
– share some of the additional benefits.

Why might **relevance** be an important factor? (p28)
– share some good examples from history of the church displaying her relevance in society.
– what might be pertinent today?

In which ways do we allow people a **voice**? (p30)
– why is that important in our communities?
– are there any pitfalls?
– what would Christ-centred leadership look like?

What place should worship take in the *ekklesia*?
– how can we encourage greater creativity?
– name different forms of the breadth of worship in union with Christ.

Discuss the statement 'Many of our songs and prayers are us asking God to give us what he has already provided us in Christ!' (p32)
– what might a different approach look like?

Why is **encounter** so vital?
– what does it deal with?
– share your experience of encounter with Jesus.
So what might a new ecclesiology look like? (p37)

We have been careful not to describe the external form or type of organisation:
– where must we start?
– what does **authenticity** look like in this respect?
– own your own story; what things might be influencing your perspective?

What are people often searching for today?
– how can the *ekklesia* meet people where they are at?
– does this give you hope for this generation?

THE NEXT CHAPTERS DEVELOP SOME OF THESE THEMES FURTHER

2. Community (p39)

Discuss the nature of the Trinity.
– where do we see this in the scriptures?
– where was the Greek term *homoousious* used: why is this critical in our understanding of salvation?

Where therefore should our starting place be in discussing *ekklesia*?
– how does the Apostle Paul describe us now?
– what are the implications for how we see people?

Discuss Baxter Kruger's statement 'In the end the whole discussion of what is church is really a footnote to 'Who is Jesus?''

Why is it still valuable to gather together?
– what essentials do we remind each other of?

What names for the devil do we read in the New Testament?
– why might that impinge on our understanding of who we are?
– in what ways do our gathered communities stand against that?

3. Sacrament (p46)

What simple act did Jesus tell us to remember him through?
– what do we understand by 'remembrance'?
– what are the amazing implications of this?
– compare some of the other names given for this meal and their meaning.

Discuss the meaning of 'sacrament'.
– what are we declaring?
– what are we not doing?

Consider some of the different ways we may celebrate this.
– does it need to be sombre affair?
– discuss some of the ways in which we encounter Christ and one another through sacrament.

Discuss the essential mystery in these things.
– how does that affect our walk of faith.
– whose faith is it?

4. Wellbeing (p51)

Is there such a thing as absolute truth?
– how should we describe it?

How should we view the scriptures?
– discuss some of the traditional views.
– where can these be challenged?
– does God mind?

What is it most important that we pass on to future generations?
– what does a healthy Christology imply?
– what therefore is the language of the Gospel?
– describe how God sees you because of this.
– how does that make you feel now?

What may be a misinterpretation of this freedom? (p53)
– what areas should we avoid?
– what warnings do the New Testament writers give?

How did the Church Fathers address some of these aberrations in 325 AD?
– what were the main errors they were addressing?
– what aspect of the nature of the Godhead comes through so clearly here.

This predates the canon of scripture!
Discuss the importance of 'the faith handed down' to the health of *ekklesia* in our day.

What might it be good to avoid in order to stay in a healthy place? (p56)
– what practices might help us in this regard?
– what provision has God made to help the church?

Discuss the 'holy wonder' of the message handed down: (p58)
— how do we understand this continuum through the ages.
— in what ways does this add to the sense of mystery in our faith?

Read out together the modern paraphrase of the Creed at the end of this section.

5. Welfare (p61)

Give some examples of how God often relates to us corporately rather than individually.
— why do you think he might do that?

Care for the poor and needy has always been a central value for the *ekklesia*.
— where has that been well demonstrated through the history of the church? Name some examples.
— in which areas do you think that the church might currently 'bear more fruit'?
— what empowers this demonstration of the Kingdom of God?

Define *koinonia*.
— how is that being demonstrated in your locality?

6. Reformation (p66)

It is 500 years since the Reformation ushered in by Luther and his friends:
– what should be understand by 'reformation'?
– why might this be happening in our day?

If we are not going to fall into the trap of reconstructing a man-made solution for the church, we need to begin in the right place!
– what will be vital in this reformation?
– where did Jesus say we find the source?

What are the dangers in trying to 'over define'?
– what does union mean to you?
– in what ways do you understand that we participate in the Divine Life?
– does this make us God? Discuss union and distinction.

How did God intend to display his genius (manifold wisdom) to every area of heavenly authority? (Eph 3:10-11)
– what sort of communities has God always envisaged then?
– why might 'rewilding' be a useful metaphor?

Why should we make space for and embrace mystery?
– how can that help us as we move forward in the 21st century?

Discuss Baxter's statement on page 71 about the 'astonished heart'.

– how has this encounter connected you to others?
– how do you see this developing?

7. Case Study: Bern West Community (p73)

What aspects of this church really stand out to you?

Ivan said, 'I've noticed also that people who are less connected to community tend to wander away from the Gospel.'
– have you seen this happen?
– what values kept the Bern Community on track?

8. Case Study: Hillside Covenant Community   (p78)

How did this church begin and what brought transformation?

How have they developed their understanding of leadership?
– what do you think about that?

What are their distinctive features?

In what areas have they needed to be more intentional?

9. Case Study: Wellsprings Community (p84)

How does Wellsprings differ from the other two examples?
– what had been the initial vision?

– what aspects have been retained?

– how differently do they now see these being expressed?

David describes their leadership model as an 'inverted pyramid'.

– in which ways can this help the church?

How does he describe the way in which they gather?

Suggestions for further reading

This list is not exhaustive, but rather contains recommendations by this author of books that he has found particularly helpful on this journey. Some of the books may be issued by more than one publisher.

On the Trinity

The Shack, by Wm. Paul Young published 2008, Hodder Windblown

The Shack Revisited, by Dr Baxter Kruger 2012, Hodder & Stoughton

The Great Dance, by Dr Baxter Kruger 2000, Regent College Publishing

Christology

The Mediation of Christ, by Thomas F. Torrance 1992 Helmers and Howard

Jesus and the Undoing of Adam, by Dr Baxter Kruger 2003, Perichoresis Press

Jesus Through Middle Eastern Eyes, by Kenneth E. Bailey 2008, SPCK

Sinners in the Hands of a Loving God, by Brian Zahnd 2017, Waterbrook

The Claim of Humanity in Christ, by Alexandra S. Radcliff 2016, Pickwick Publications

Kingdom, Grace, Judgment: Paradox, Outrage, and Vindication in the Parables of Jesus, by Robert Farrar Capon 1985, Eerdmans

Mystery and union

Mystical Union, by John Crowder 2010, Sons of Thunder Ministries & Publications

Cosmos Reborn, by John Crowder 2013, Sons of Thunder Ministries & Publications

Chosen for Paradise, by John Crowder 2014, Sons of Thunder Ministries & Publications

The nature of the Father

Unspoken Sermons, by George MacDonald (1824-1905) available in various editions

A More Christlike God, by Bradley Jersak 2016, Plain Truth Ministries

A More Christlike Word, by Bradley Jersak 2021, Whitaker House

God of Covenant, God of Grace, by Colin Symes 2021, Amazon

General spirituality

The Practice of the Presence of God, Brother Lawrence (1611 -91) available in various editions

Revelations of Divine Love, Julian of Norwich (1342-1416) available in various editions

New Seeds of Contemplation, by Thomas Merton 1961, New Directions

Worship, Community and the Triune God of Grace, by James B. Torrance 1994, Paternoster Press

Listening for the Heartbeat of God: A Celtic Spirituality, by Philip Newell 1977, SPCK

Grace for the Contemplative Parent, Lily Crowder 2013, Sons of Thunder Ministries & Publications

Out of the Embers: Faith After the Great Deconstruction, by Bradley Jersak 2022, Whitaker House

High on God, by Matt Spinks 2018, Firehouse Projects

Unveiled Horizon: Reflections on the Nature of God, by Bill Vanderbush 2022, Faith Mountain Publishing

Leaving and Finding Jesus, Jason Clark 2022, Amazon

The Secret: What You Know But Never Knew, by Dr Baxter Kruger 2022, Perichoresis Press

Ultimate Rest: The Essence of the Beautiful Gospel, by David Hewitt 2024 Wellsprings Community, Amazon

TAKING IT FURTHER

If you wish to develop this conversation you may wish to join in with conferences and online discussions that take place regularly.
For further details on these and other relevant events, email:

info@wellsprings.uk.net

including some details about yourself and your situation.

Wellsprings Community is based on the eastern edge of Edinburgh, Scotland, UK. The address is 71 Whitehill Street, Newcraighall, Edinburgh EH21 8QZ.

People are welcome to visit and we may have a guest room available.

Visit our website for up-to-date information:

www.wellsprings.uk.net

THE FLOWERING TREE
Stained glass window at the Church of St Mary the Virgin, a parish church
in the village of Iffley, Oxfordshire, England *(Photo: Simon Hodge)*

www.ingramcontent.com/pod-product-compliance
Lightning Source LLC
Chambersburg PA
CBHW060016050426
42448CB00012B/2779